D0783932

A PRIVATE FUNCTION

also by Alan Bennett

A PRIVATE FUNCTION
A screenplay

ALAN BENNETT
From a story by Alan Bennett and Malcolm Mowbray

faber and faber
LONDON · BOSTON

in association with Hand Made Films

First published in 1984
by Faber and Faber Limited
3 Queen Square London WC1N 3AU

Phototypeset by Wyvern Typesetting Limited, Bristol
Printed in Great Britain by
Whitstable Litho Limited, Whitstable

©HandMade Films (Productions) Limited, 1984

British Library Cataloguing in Publication Data
Bennett, Alan
 A private function.
 I. Title
 822'.914 PR6052.E5
ISBN 0-571-13571-4

INTRODUCTION

'A steam-filled bathroom. The camera pans along a shelf of
toilet requisites, shampoo, talcum powder, toothbrushes in a
glass, and slowly down towards the bath. Through the steam
we see what appears to be a plump, white arm hanging
elegantly over the side. In the bath is a dead pig.'

The idea for *A Private Function* came from Malcolm
Mowbray. He wanted to make a film about the immediate post-
war years, when rationing and food shortages were more severe
than at any time during the war. Though the pig in the bath
was an actual incident in the lives of his in-laws, who raised
and killed a clandestine pig and scalded it in their own bath,
the years just after the war were for Malcolm an historical
period. I could remember them, though not with much
nostalgia. My father was a butcher and the weekly worry that
his allotted supply would not be enough to cover the
requirements of his registered customers eventually landed him
in hospital with a duodenal ulcer.

I dare say Leeds, where we lived, was no more corrupt than
anywhere else; certainly there were quite a few butchers in our
neighbourhood who were on the twist, and everyone knew who
they were. Though Leeds is a much larger place than the town
in the film there was the same sense that, rationing
notwithstanding, some people were still doing very nicely,
thank you. The same must have been true in country areas. I
know of one village that was regularly visited by a hearse, the
visits seemingly unrelated to the death rate. Stopped one day
by a Ministry of Food inspector it was found to be carrying a
coffin packed with pork . . . an incident far too theatrical to be
put in the film, life as so often more over the top than anything
one could invent. But ask anybody in the village today about
pigs in that period and they still look over their shoulder before
replying. So, though the central incident of the theft of the pig

may nowadays seem far-fetched, I don't think it would have
been then. Though whether a fully qualified chiropodist, even
when married, like Gilbert, to a distant relative of Lady
Macbeth, would descend to such a deed is another matter.

Those days are hard to recall now and the newsreel that
starts the film was put in to inform as much as to entertain.
Sticklers for historical accuracy will probably spot that the
marriage of Princess Elizabeth to the Duke of Edinburgh took
place in November, a November in our film when the trees are
in full leaf and the countryside bathed in warm sunshine.

We filmed most of the story on location in Ilkley and
Barnoldswick, happening to find in the latter place an empty
parade of shops with, as a centrepiece, a disused cinema. Many
of the countryside scenes are in Wharfedale around Bolton

8

Abbey. Sutcliff's farm was Laund House, an idyllic spot above the Wharfe where Beatrix Potter used to stay, the kitchen garden still overrun with rabbits but with no Mr McGregor to say them nay.

Betty was played by three different pigs, not in order to comply with the requirements of Equity or the RSPCA but because each pig had different skills. One was a good runner but shy in company; another could climb stairs but would not sit still, and the third, while much the most photogenic, had a black patch on its back that had to be painted out before it went in front of the camera. The lynx-eyed continuity buff will note that Betty may seem to vary in size from shot to shot. She does. The only way to persuade the pigs to perform was by constant feeding; they therefore grew at an alarming rate. Since the film was not shot in sequence this can mean that Betty is quite portly in one shot, suddenly slim in the next.

There are obvious hazards of working with a pig and they are not all that different from the hazards of stealing one. Toilet training is not their forte and one of the unsung members of the unit was an unemployed Ilkley boy whose job it was to follow Betty round with a bucket and kitchen roll. The slightest quiver of the porcine sphincter and he was there poised with his pail. It was his first job in Mrs Thatcher's New Model England and he deserves a credit with the director and the stars.

There is no such thing as a good script, only a good film and I'm conscious that my scripts often read better than they play. Of some scenes in *A Private Function* this is certainly true. It is easy to write 'The pig smiles' or 'The pig trots dutifully after him' and quite another to persuade the creature to do so. So in any scene involving the pig the script tends to be a statement of intention rather than a description of what actually happens.

Pigs are undoubtedly intelligent creatures and nothing if not determined. The squeals of a pig being persuaded to go where it doesn't want to or to do anything (which is most things apart from eating) that it doesn't want to do is the sound of angry,

9

frustrated *will*. By the exercise of patience and nerve (time always running out) Malcolm Mowbray generally managed to get some kind of convincing behaviour on film. But in the scene where Gilbert has to entice the pig into his car and drive away with it we all but failed. The scene as shot is just about convincing, but in ideal circumstances (more money, more time) the sequence should have been longer, happier and in the end more triumphant. But it was a night shoot, the woods where we were filming thick with wild garlic and the appeal of the tastiest morsel blunted.

In the end we were thankful to have got the pig into the car at all and had to abandon the scenes of Gilbert driving along with it as described in the script. Once in the car it had been no joke. With one trotter in his crotch and the other round his neck Michael Palin compared it to being in the car with an overweight and over-amorous landlady. And like landladies they are, trotting naked over the linoleum in their little high heels, delicate and fastidious, their quivering bottoms wonderful to see. 'Oh yes,' said Denholm Elliott, 'once that thing gets its snout into the lens I can see none of us are going to get a look-in.' And not merely its snout.

In the end the pig is killed. It wasn't our pig admittedly, all three of it now living in retirement in Sussex. Still a pig was killed, several if one counts the carcasses in the bed and in the wardrobe. The final credits sequence, in which Gilbert and Allardyce fondle their newly acquired piglet was put in to take the edge off Betty's death. But of course that piglet too will be dead by now. I haven't eaten pork since, though without thinking this a sensible, sufficient or even logical response. The scene of the pig in the bath that started it all seemed, when shot, to hold things up and was cut from the finished film. That's often the way. Still, it was a favourite scene so I've left it in the script as something that did once happen, even if not in the film we made out of it.

ALAN BENNETT

July 1984

A PRIVATE FUNCTION

The year 1947 was one of repeated disappointments and steady perseverance, introduced by a winter of exceptional cold aggravated by a breakdown in fuel and electricity supplies. It ended on a note of almost unrelieved austerity. Supplies to the home consumer were cut to a minimum as a result of the virtual exhaustion of the nation's dollar resources, and an energetic production drive was initiated.

All political parties were as one in demanding a return to the "Dunkirk Spirit" of sacrifice and in promising the country a long period of hard exertion and small reward. The marriage of Princess Elizabeth to Prince Philip, Duke of Edinburgh, on November 20th, though celebrated with restrained festivity, came as a welcome tonic to the public spirit and was an occasion of joy throughout Britain.

Britannica's Book of the Year, 1948

CHARACTERS

GILBERT CHILVERS

JOYCE CHILVERS

MOTHER

LOCKWOOD

MRS ALLARDYCE

ALLARDYCE

DR SWABY

VERONICA

MRS METCALF

MR METCALF

WORMOLD

INSPECTOR NOBLE

PC PENNY

MRS METCALF'S FATHER

MRS FORBES

NUTTALL

ERNEST

BARRACLOUGH

DOROTHY

WOMAN

PAINTER

SUTCLIFF

MRS SUTCLIFF

PRESTON

PAINTER'S BOY

HOTEL MANAGER

MERVIN

MRS TURNBULL

The première of *A Private Function* took place on 21
November 1984 at the Odeon Cinema, Haymarket, London.
The cast of the film is as follows:

GILBERT CHILVERS	Michael Palin
JOYCE CHILVERS	Maggie Smith
MOTHER	Liz Smith
LOCKWOOD	John Normington
MRS ALLARDYCE	Alison Steadman
ALLARDYCE	Richard Griffiths
DR SWABY	Denholm Elliott
VERONICA	Amanda Gregan
MRS METCALF	Susan Porrett
MR METCALF	Charles McKeown
WORMOLD	Bill Paterson
INSPECTOR NOBLE	Jim Carter
PC PENNY	Reece Dinsdale
MRS METCALF'S FATHER	Donald Eccles
MRS FORBES	Rachel Davies

NUTTALL	Pete Postlethwaite
ERNEST	Eli Woods
BARRACLOUGH	Don Estelle
DOROTHY	Gilly Coman
WOMAN	Maggie Ollerenshaw
PAINTER	Bernard Wrigley
SUTCLIFF	Tony Haygarth
MRS SUTCLIFF	Eileen O'Brien
PRESTON	Philip Wileman
PAINTER'S BOY	Lee Daley
HOTEL MANAGER	Denys Hawthorne
MERVIN	David Morgan
MRS TURNBULL	Paula Tilbrook
Music	John Du Prez
Executive Producers	George Harrison
	Denis O'Brien
Producer	Mark Shivas
Director	Malcolm Mowbray

I. INT. ARCADIA CINEMA. AFTERNOON

As the title of the film fades from the screen the introductory credits roll, in the type and style of a late forties movie. As they give way to the crowing cockerel of Pathé News we realize we are in a cinema.

NEWSREEL COMMENTATOR: Nineteen forty-seven and Austerity Britain gets a longed-for whiff of glamour as preparations for the wedding of Her Royal Highness Princess Elizabeth get into full swing.

(*At the back of the stalls* JOYCE *and her* MOTHER *are coming in.* JOYCE *is a thin genteel woman, given to suffering. Her* MOTHER *is the woman who has made her so. As they come in the door* JOYCE *whispers:*)

JOYCE: Mind where you're going, Mother. There's a step.

(MOTHER *stumbles.*)

MOTHER: You didn't say there was a step.

(JOYCE *and* MOTHER *go down the aisle as the urgent voice of the* NEWSREEL COMMENTATOR *lets us into a secret: the wedding cake for the forthcoming nuptials was made with ingredients supplied by Australian Girl Guides.*

JOYCE *and* MOTHER *are now seated and looking up at the screen, though at a curiously acute angle. Indeed the screen seems almost above their heads.*)

It hurts your neck here.

(*Now the newsreel begins a fresh item: the announcement of a cut in the bacon ration. We see a week's food rations displayed on a table. There hardly seems enough for a square meal. A close-up of the bacon ration reveals it as only two rashers and now a hand comes in and removes one of them: the bacon ration has been halved.* JOYCE *looks at* MOTHER. *The halving of the bacon ration seems something of a last straw.* JOYCE's *rig-out contrasts strangely with* MOTHER's.

MOTHER *is in a dowdy coat with a fur tippet,* JOYCE *is resplendent in a turquoise sequinned number with matching accessories. It seems a fancy frock for the afternoon cinema. The* NEWSREEL COMMENTATOR *is now explaining how similar shortages in France have led to a flourishing black market. The implication is that in Britain there is no such thing.*)

NEWSREEL COMMENTATOR: (*Winding up*) In Britain for the moment our minds are on happier things.

(*There is another shot of the royal couple as* JOYCE *begins to get restive.*)

JOYCE: Go on, Mother. Sit on your seat.

MOTHER: (*Looking round*) Where?

JOYCE: (*Panicking*) Go *on*. I'm going up. Oh, Mother.

(*We cut to a wide shot of the cinema as the curtains close on the screen and* JOYCE *rises to light and glory at the console of the cinema organ. As she rises* JOYCE *looks over her shoulder and flashes a beaming smile at the audience. The effect is somewhat spoilt by the dour figure of* MOTHER *still sitting beside her. She too looks round but does not smile.*)

2. EXT. COUNTRY ROAD. DAY

A moorland road on the edge of a small northern town. Joyce's husband, GILBERT CHILVERS, *cycles along on a heavy, old-fashioned bike. He is a pleasant, mild-looking man in his thirties. In his bike basket is a little black bag. Piano music, hesitant in the playing and cheap and romantic in tone, begins to intrude upon this scene.*

3. INT. CHILVERS' HOUSE. DAY

JOYCE *is looking with somewhat self-conscious melancholy through the window of their semi-detached house. The cheap and romantic piano music now falters and stops.* JOYCE *half turns. Sitting at the piano is* VERONICA ALLARDYCE, *a child in pigtails. They look at one another and* JOYCE *closes her eyes in despair.* VERONICA *is beginning to practise her piece again when the door bell goes.*

4. EXT. CHILVERS' HOUSE. DAY

A DELIVERY MAN *waits at the door with an ungainly parcel. Joyce's* MOTHER *watches him. Stood in the garden, she is eating a sandwich. As* JOYCE *opens the door she puts the sandwich behind her back.*

JOYCE: (*having signed for parcel*) Mother. Are you eating?

(MOTHER *shakes her head.* JOYCE *closes the door and* MOTHER *takes another bite of the sandwich.*)

5. EXT. COUNTRY ROAD. DAY
GILBERT *stops to eat his packed lunch, with a view stretched out before him. He pours some coffee from the thermos, and opens his newspaper which is headlined "Bacon down again".* GILBERT *sighs and opens his lunch box. Wonderingly he takes out a couple of crochet hooks and half a crocheted dishcloth. There are no sandwiches. Looking even more glum* GILBERT *takes an apple from his pocket and begins to peel it with a small surgical-looking knife.*

6. INT. CHILVERS' HOUSE. DAY
GILBERT *is seen cycling away down the drive. As the lace curtain held up from the window is let down, we see that the lady watching* GILBERT *leave has a stocking crumpled in her hand.*

7. EXT. STREETS. DAY
GILBERT *bikes along, passing several queues outside shops, one of which is Barraclough's butcher's.*

8. EXT. THE PARADE. DAY
Dismounting, GILBERT *wheels his bike along the Parade. As he passes the cinema entrance on the Parade, we hear Grieg's Piano Concerto from the film* The Seventh Veil, *playing inside.*
GILBERT *pauses by Hewson's wireless shop, where a* COUPLE *are regarding one of the new televisions, which is displayed in the window. A notice on the cabinet, which dwarfs the screen, tells people that they can "See the Royal Wedding Here". The* MAN *throws a cigarette packet down in the doorway of the small empty shop next door. Gilbert looks askance. Moving into this doorway he picks up the man's rubbish as he looks at a "Let" sign on the door. A look of satisfaction grows on his face.*

9. EXT. ALLARDYCES' HOUSE. DAY
There are two cars parked in the drive. A HANDYMAN *in an old khaki shirt is playing a hose over the first car. A lace curtain drawn back suggests someone is watching the* HANDYMAN *or* GILBERT, *who, having admired the cars, parks his bike.*

10. INT. ALLARDYCE'S STUDY. DAY
Three middle-aged men are in the room. ALLARDYCE *is an*
accountant, LOCKWOOD *a solicitor and* SWABY *a medical*
practitioner. ALLARDYCE *is a plump, genuine soul,* LOCKWOOD
is sour and small-minded, not genuine at all. DR SWABY *is a*
thoroughgoing shit. They all have sheets of paper on which are lists
of names.
LOCKWOOD: (*Reading from his list*) Coddington. Jezzard.
Ibbotson.

> (*The doorbell rings.* ALLARDYCE *looks up and from his point*
> *of vision we see a plump woman's arm reach in and close the*
> *study door.*)
> (*Continuing*) Starkey. Mrs R. Jack Palmer.
> (ALLARDYCE *is still looking at the door that has closed.*)

11. INT. ALLARDYCES' SITTING ROOM. DAY
Prosperously furnished. The most prominent object in the room is an
early television set, screen about nine inches wide, in a large walnut
console. On top of it is a bowl of bananas. MRS ALLARDYCE, *a*
fleshy and masterful middle-aged woman, is in the act of lifting her
skirt to undo her suspender, turning away from GILBERT *slightly*
in order to do so.
MRS ALLARDYCE: You're younger than I'd been led to
expect. However.

> (GILBERT *doesn't say anything.*)
> Mrs Lockwood says she's a new woman.
GILBERT: Have you a newspaper, Mrs Allardyce? This is a
good carpet.
MRS ALLARDYCE: Wholesale from Halifax, of course it is.

12. INT. ALLARDYCE'S STUDY. DAY
LOCKWOOD *is still reading out his list, with* DR SWABY *repeating*
the names in confirmation as he ticks them off.
LOCKWOOD: Gibson. Proctor. Chalmers-Smith. Major
Hopkinson.

ALLARDYCE: (*Smiling happily and ticking off a name*) Great
    minds think alike.
LOCKWOOD: Sutcliff?
    (*Pause.*)
DR SWABY: He might not want to come.
LOCKWOOD: *She* will.
    (MRS ALLARDYCE *comes in, one stocking on, one off.*)
MRS ALLARDYCE: Paper, Henry?
    (ALLARDYCE *is sitting on it.*)
ALLARDYCE: It's today's.
    (*She takes it.*)
MRS ALLARDYCE: And? (*Meaning "What of it?"*)
    (*She goes.* DR SWABY *and* LOCKWOOD *exchange pitying
    looks.*)
LOCKWOOD: (*Continuing*) Dickinson.
DR SWABY: Dickinson.

13. INT. ALLARDYCES' SITTING ROOM. DAY
MRS ALLARDYCE: Where do you want me?
    (*She sits on a chair and* GILBERT, *opening the paper, places
    it under her feet. He then turns to his case. Glancing down*
    MRS ALLARDYCE *finds that her naked foot is on a portrait of
    the bridegroom-to-be, Lieutenant Mountbatten. Thinking this is
    lèse-majesté she removes the page, only to find she now has her
    foot on some other royal person. This too she removes, settling
    eventually for the front page with its headline "Bacon Down
    Again".* GILBERT *takes hold of her foot.*)
    My other little man died. He used to say that a foot told
    him more than a face.
GILBERT: Well, you've got quite a lot of hard skin. And this
    is a chilblain.
    (MRS ALLARDYCE *plainly doesn't feel this is much insight
    into the real her.*)
    Are you on your feet a great deal?
MRS ALLARDYCE: My husband's an accountant. It's one
    function after another.

(She reaches over and gets a cigarette from the box and as GILBERT *bends over her feet she leans back and takes a luxurious drag. Somewhere in the house a comfortable-sounding middle-class clock chimes.)*

14. INT. ALLARDYCE'S STUDY. DAY

ALLARDYCE *is now reading out his list.*

ALLARDYCE: Jezzard.

DR SWABY: Had Jezzard.

ALLARDYCE: Sorry. Wainwright.

(LOCKWOOD *pulls a face.*)

Brierley?

LOCKWOOD: It wants to be a bit select, Henry. Their daughter was a GI bride.

DR SWABY: Only just. Six months pregnant when I examined her.

ALLARDYCE: She was a Sunday School teacher.

DR SWABY: The state of her private parts told a different story, Henry. This is royalty. It's a pure and unspoiled couple.

ALLARDYCE: Goodman?

(There is a slightly more awkward silence.)

DR SWABY: He's not on my list.

ALLARDYCE: They're very well off.

DR SWABY: Well apart from anything else, Henry, think what we shall be having to eat. *(Pause.)* Oink-oink.

ALLARDYCE: Oh.

(DR SWABY *and* LOCKWOOD *exchange looks of long-suffering contempt. Someone starts to play the piano badly, the same tune we have heard at the Chilvers' house.* ALLARDYCE *gets up and opens the door.*)

Not now, Veronica.

15. INT. ALLARDYCES' SITTING ROOM. DAY

MRS ALLARDYCE: *(Calling)* She's got to practise sometime.

(The piano starts again. MRS ALLARDYCE *picks a chocolate*

and takes a bite. Not liking its taste she drops the rest of the chocolate, and it lands among the clippings and shavings of hard skin on the newspaper. Looking up from it GILBERT *continues to clip her toenails.* MRS ALLARDYCE *smooths the stocking she has on.*)

Nylons. Henry gets them. Grateful clients.

GILBERT: (*Cutting her big toenail*) Bad for the feet.

(*The big toenail clipping flies off.* MRS ALLARDYCE *looks up as it "pings" off a vase.*)

MRS ALLARDYCE: (*Recovering*) Good for the morale. I think we've let some toenail go on the carpet.

GILBERT: Beg pardon. This is a bit hand to mouth. But I'll have my own surgery soon. I've got premises on the Parade.

MRS ALLARDYCE: Oh, the Parade. Umpteen opportunities for the go-ahead young man these days. The war killed so many off. And you're married to Veronica's piano teacher.

GILBERT: Yes.

MRS ALLARDYCE: You're not wearing a ring.

GILBERT: No. Tiny bits of skin and scurf from people's feet tend to collect under it.

MRS ALLARDYCE: Oh. My other little man was married, though his wife was bedridden. Life.

(ALLARDYCE *enters. He does not see* GILBERT *as he is hidden below the level of the chair.*)

ALLARDYCE: Still a long way to go with the invites. Have we anything tasty we could give Dr Swaby for his supper? You know what he's like.

(MRS ALLARDYCE *mutely indicates the presence of* GILBERT.)

(*Peering round the chair*) Ah!

MRS ALLARDYCE: Steak?

(ALLARDYCE *is going, when he stops and returns, having seen something.*)

ALLARDYCE: Are you not eating that?

MRS ALLARDYCE: They're marzipan. You don't like marzipan.
(ALLARDYCE *nevertheless reaches down, and it's only then that we realize he's referring to the half-eaten chocolate lying among all the nail clippings etc. on the paper. He retrieves it from under* GILBERT's *nose and goes out, carrying it in front of him in a way that suggests he isn't going to eat it. Pause.*)
We generally have our main meal at night.

16. INT. ALLARDYCES' HALL. DAY
VERONICA *can be seen practising in a further room.* ALLARDYCE *is stood by the doorway but he is looking off. Emerging from the toilet,* DR SWABY *joins* ALLARDYCE. *He looks in at* VERONICA *with stony indifference.* ALLARDYCE *shows* DR SWABY *the half-eaten chocolate and is about to say something when the sitting-room door begins to open and* DR SWABY *hustles him unceremoniously back into the study.* MRS ALLARDYCE *leads* GILBERT *out of the sitting room towards the front door.*
VERONICA: I hate Mrs Chilvers.
MRS ALLARDYCE: (*Sweetly*) No, you don't. This is Mr Chilvers. Children! You don't have any?
GILBERT: No.
MRS ALLARDYCE: Very wise.
(*Looking out of the house, past* MRS ALLARDYCE, *we see* GILBERT *mounting his bike.*)

17. EXT. METCALF'S BUTCHER'S SHOP. EVENING
We see GILBERT *arriving on his bike.* MR METCALF *is just letting the blinds down having shut the shop.* GILBERT *knocks and* MR METCALF *peeps out, then lets him in. As the shop door closes behind* GILBERT, *the camera pulls back and we see a black-gloved hand drumming impatiently on a steering wheel.*

18. INT. METCALF'S SHOP. EVENING
GILBERT *goes through the back of the shop, where lights, beasts' heads, etc., are hanging up and* MR METCALF *points him up the*

stairs into the house, while he starts putting his stock back into the fridge.

19. INT. METCALFS' LIVING ROOM. EVENING
Less moneyed than the ALLARDYCES, *but nicely off too.* MRS
METCALF, *a volatile ferret of a woman, talking all the time.*
GILBERT *is already on the floor, doing her feet.* MR METCALF *is standing in the doorway watching.*

MRS METCALF: Heartbreaking, these days, butchering. Meat
  ration at one and tenpence, what can you do with that?
  His stomach's on a knife edge.
  (MR METCALF *goes.*)
  And he's the only one who's straight. There's two other
  butchers and they're both on the twist. He comes in on a
  night, sits at that table and his face is grey. You've got
  some nice thick hair.
  (*There is a loud banging at the door. She gets up and hobbles
  to the window. Below, in the shop,* MR METCALF *is scooting
  back from the door in a crouched position.*)
MR METCALF: Gestapo!
MRS METCALF: Oh, blood and sand!
  (*She rushes off into the kitchen as the banging on the shop
  door is renewed.* GILBERT *is nonplussed.* MRS METCALF
  runs back in with a side of pork, watched by the amazed
  GILBERT. *As she rushes to the stairs down to the shop,* MR
  METCALF *is rushing up them, also carrying a side of pork.*)
MR METCALF: Not down here, you fool. Get it upstairs.
  (*They rush out, upstairs. The banging continues with*
  GILBERT *nonplussed. He gets up and half goes to the door,
  but doesn't know what to do. The letterbox is pushed back.*)
WORMOLD: (*Out of vision*) You. Open this door.
GILBERT: I can't. I'm the chiropodist.
INSPECTOR NOBLE: (*Out of vision*) This is the police.
  Open this door.
(GILBERT *starts trying to.*)
GILBERT: It's a funny lock.

(MRS METCALF *comes in from the stairs.*)

MRS METCALF: (*Supremely calm*) Is there somebody at the
    door? One moment.
    (*She opens the door and* INSPECTOR NOBLE *and* PC
    PENNY *rush in, followed by the more sinister, black-gloved
    figure of* WORMOLD, *the Ministry of Food Inspector.*
    WORMOLD *should be Scots or from Birmingham. He is not
    local.*)

WORMOLD: Upstairs.

MRS METCALF: You will find the shop downstairs.

WORMOLD: Upstairs.
    (PC PENNY, *a young policeman, and* WORMOLD *are about
    to go upstairs.*)

MRS METCALF: Excuse me. This is my house.
    (*She leads the way, leaving* INSPECTOR NOBLE *and*
    GILBERT *staring at one another.* NOBLE *admires himself in
    the mirror, seemingly unconcerned.*)

20. INT. METCALFS' LANDING. EVENING

WORMOLD *knocks on a door.*

MR METCALF: (*Out of vision*) I'm on the toilet.

WORMOLD: I can wait.
    (MR METCALF *comes out immediately.* WORMOLD *goes in
    and comes out empty-handed.* MR METCALF *goes back
    downstairs while* WORMOLD *continues to search the house.*)

21. INT. METCALFS' LIVING ROOM. EVENING

INSPECTOR NOBLE *and* GILBERT *are there.*

MR METCALF: (*Muttering to* NOBLE) What happened to the
    telephone?

INSPECTOR NOBLE: He's a law unto himself.
    (*We should see at some point Wormold's attaché case, with
    "Ministry of Food" stamped on it.*)

22. INT. METCALFS' LANDING. EVENING

MRS METCALF *knocks on a bedroom door.*

MRS METCALF: Father? (*To* WORMOLD) Don't get him excited. He has trouble with his waterworks.

(MRS METCALF'S FATHER, *a small anxious head on a pillow, watches them as they look round the room and then go out. The search party goes into another bedroom.* PC PENNY *looks under the bed, then looks in the wardrobe.*)

PC PENNY: Nothing here.

WORMOLD: Come out.

(PC PENNY *makes room and* WORMOLD, *watched by* PENNY, *flicks along the row of coats and dresses hanging up. Among them is a side of pork.*)

23. INT. METCALFS' LIVING ROOM. EVENING

WORMOLD *comes down first, followed by* PC PENNY *with the side of pork.* MRS METCALF *is hovering behind.*

INSPECTOR NOBLE: Dear oh dear. Dear oh dear.

MRS METCALF (To PC PENNY): Put a bit of something under that, love.

(*She slips a cloth between the pork and* PC PENNY'S *uniform.*)

The grease'll go all over your uniform. Your mam'll play pop.

(PC PENNY *seems to be lingering. He is eyeing a single banana in a dish on the table. The others continue out.*)

PC PENNY: Mrs Metcalf?

MRS METCALF: What, love?

PC PENNY: Are you wanting that banana?

MRS METCALF: (*Apologetically*) I am, love, I'm planning a trifle.

(PC PENNY *goes, carrying the pork. The procession goes out to the car, watched by* MRS METCALF. *She closes the door and then beckons* GILBERT *to follow her upstairs.*)

24. INT. METCALFS' LANDING. EVENING

MRS METCALF *leads* GILBERT *into her father's room.*

MRS METCALF'S FATHER: Your mam feels cold, Dorcas.

MRS METCALF: It's not surprising. She died in 1937.
(*She pulls back the bedclothes and the* OLD MAN *is embracing a side of pork.*)
Can you manage that?
(GILBERT *begins to lift it gingerly.*)
See.
(*She yanks it off the bed, then puts it in* GILBERT's *arms.*)
Downstairs.

25. INT. METCALFS' LIVING ROOM. EVENING
GILBERT *comes down into the living room,* MRS METCALF *following.*
MRS METCALF: Down again.

26. INT. METCALF'S SHOP. EVENING
GILBERT *manoeuvres the side of pork down the stairs, through the*

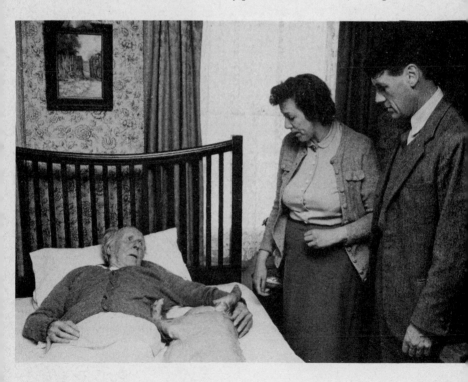

beasts' heads and bits of offal and into the big walk-in fridge.
Following her directions, he hangs it up and comes out. MRS
METCALF *closes the fridge door.*
MRS METCALF: Well, don't look at me. People have to live.
You'd better come and finish my feet.

27. INT. CHILVERS' DINING ROOM. EVENING
The room, like the house, is excessively tidy. JOYCE *watches while*
GILBERT *unwraps the parcel we saw being delivered earlier.*
JOYCE: Pork? In bed? They want horsewhipping. We never
saw any of it. When did we last have pork? And it wasn't
clean. I've seen a cat on that counter.
(GILBERT *reveals a large porcelain foot from a box inside the*
parcel's brown wrapping paper.)

GILBERT: What do you think?

JOYCE: I suppose I've now got to start looking for another butcher. Wash it. It's probably filthy. What was this meeting?

(GILBERT *carries the foot to the sink in the kitchen to wash it.* JOYCE *follows.*)

GILBERT: It's a dinner they're getting up for the Royal Wedding.

JOYCE: No need to ask if we were invited.

GILBERT: We don't want to be going to dinners. What do we want to be going to dinners for?

JOYCE: To meet people, that's what for. How else are you going to get on? It's dripping, Gilbert. It's dripping! What was the house like?

GILBERT: A palace. They were having steak for their supper.

JOYCE: Steak! You were going to take this town, Gilbert.

GILBERT: I'm a chiropodist, Joyce, not a Panzer division. Look. Jesus.

JOYCE: I beg your pardon.

GILBERT: Washing the feet.

(JOYCE *turns away with a pained expression as* MOTHER *comes in.*)

MOTHER: Have I had my tea?

JOYCE: Eat some of your nougat, love.

MOTHER: You don't give me my proper rations. He has my rations.

(MOTHER *is transfixed, staring at* GILBERT. *She can only see the toes but the foot that he is drying looks horribly big. She turns and hurries out of the kitchen.*)

GILBERT: (*Unaware*) She had my sandwiches again today.

JOYCE: She, Gilbert? She? She as you call her knitted you a lovely Balaclava helmet but we don't talk about that.

GILBERT: It doesn't have an opening for my mouth.

JOYCE: She's 74.

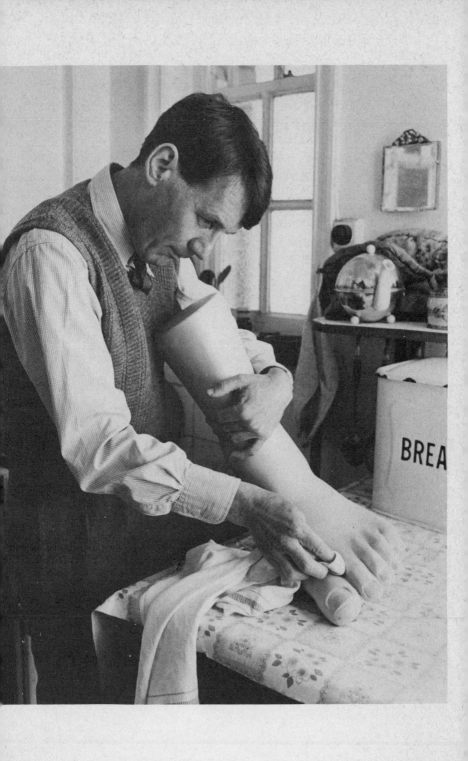

28. INT. POLICE STATION. NIGHT

We glimpse INSPECTOR NOBLE *sitting at his desk slowly taking balls out of his mouth. In another room* PC PENNY *comes upon* WORMOLD *about to paint the pork with an indelible green dye.* PC PENNY *rushes into Noble's office.*

PC PENNY: He's going to paint the pork.

> (*Balls cascade from* INSPECTOR NOBLE's *mouth and we realize that in his spare moments the* INSPECTOR *is a conjuror. This has nothing to do with the plot.* NOBLE *hastens out with* PC PENNY *following.*)

INSPECTOR NOBLE: We can do that, Mr Wormold. You've done enough for one day.

WORMOLD: No. This is the part I enjoy. This means it's unfit for human consumption.

PC PENNY: Why?

WORMOLD: Who killed it? Where?

> (INSPECTOR NOBLE *and* PC PENNY *exchange looks.*)
> I used to like painting when I was little. My mother wanted me to be an artist.

PC PENNY: (*Looking at the pork*) What a waste.

WORMOLD: No. I'd never have been any good.

29. INT. MRS FORBES'S HOUSE (WORMOLD'S LODGINGS). NIGHT

MRS FORBES, *a well-set-up middle-aged lady, is sitting behind the table in the kitchen. Hearing the outside door close, she waits for a moment and then goes out into the passage.* WORMOLD *is hanging up his coat, very neatly.* MRS FORBES *watches him fondly.*

MRS FORBES: Another day.

> (WORMOLD *smiles faintly then comes down the passage to his room.*)
> Nothing from Kuala Lumpur.
> (WORMOLD *pauses over this and then is about to go into his cheerless room when he turns.*)

WORMOLD: Mrs Forbes. Your information was correct. You'll be happy to know an arrest was made and charges are being preferred.

(MRS FORBES *comes back into the kitchen looking anything but happy.*)

30. EXT. NUTTALL'S BUTCHER'S SHOP, REAR. NIGHT
A police car pulls up in the alley. The engine and lights cut out and it sits in the dark.

31. INT. NUTTALL'S SHOP. NIGHT
NUTTALL *is standing waiting, his coat on over his butcher's coat.* ERNEST, *his ancient boy, is sitting on the counter, smoking. There is a knock at the back door.* ERNEST *answers it and* INSPECTOR NOBLE *and* PC PENNY *come in,* PC PENNY *bearing the pork in a blanket.*

NUTTALL: I'm waiting.

INSPECTOR NOBLE: He's just this minute gone.

(PC PENNY *uncovers the green pork.*)

NUTTALL: Oh dear, oh dear, oh dear. No, no, no, no.

ERNEST: No, no.

NUTTALL: I've told you. I want it prior to the painting.

INSPECTOR NOBLE: You don't know what he's like. He's a demon.

(NUTTALL *examines the pork more closely.*)

NUTTALL: It's dogmeat is this.

ERNEST: Dogmeat is that.

PC PENNY: We did try.

INSPECTOR NOBLE: We did.

(NUTTALL *grudgingly cuts them some chops, one for* PC PENNY, *two for* INSPECTOR NOBLE, *then even more grudgingly adding a third to* INSPECTOR NOBLE'S. *He then ushers them out of the back door and locks it.*)

ERNEST: Dogmeat is that.

NUTTALL: Dogmeat be buggered. Get your coat off.
(ERNEST *struggles out of his coat.*)
Bath (*Puts a zinc bath down.*) Bucket.
(ERNEST *hands him a bucket.*)
Bleach. (*Wallops in a lot of bleach.*) Now then. Get
scrubbing.

32. INT. ALLARDYCES' DINING ROOM. NIGHT
A lavish meal at which MR *and* MRS ALLARDYCE, DR SWABY
and LOCKWOOD *are present.*
MRS ALLARDYCE: How's your steak?
LOCKWOOD: Just right.
(*An indeterminate noise halts all cutlery but* DR SWABY's.
Can he have farted?)
MRS ALLARDYCE: (*Breaking their pause*) More sprouts, Dr
Swaby?

33. INT. CHILVERS' DINING ROOM. NIGHT
JOYCE, GILBERT *and* MOTHER *are eating a sparse meal of
luncheon meat, lettuce and one tomato. They eat in silence,*
GILBERT *and* MOTHER *heartily,* JOYCE *daintily.*
GILBERT: I saw another verruca today. Gone the wrong way
again. They will hack at them with razor blades.
JOYCE: Don't bring feet to the table, Gilbert. And there's
crumbs cascading on to this carpet.
GILBERT: You have to wait until they come to a head. Then
it's a piece of cake.
(JOYCE *gives up any attempt to eat.*)
Still, Mrs Roach's ingrowing toenail seems to have turned
the corner. Thanked me profusely. Gave me a macaroon.
JOYCE: (*Passionately*) A macaroon! A macaroon! We're better
than this, Gilbert.
GILBERT: Better than what?
(JOYCE *sighs.*)
Are you not eating your Spam?

36

(MOTHER *is on to it like a rat, long before* GILBERT *reaches it.*)

Listen, Joyce. Once I'm into these premises on the Parade then it'll be different. They'll be rolling up in their cars. We'll be going out to functions, having steak.

JOYCE: It's not just steak, Gilbert. Can't you see. It's status.

MOTHER: Is there any?

JOYCE: What?

MOTHER: Taties?

JOYCE: It breaks your heart.

34. INT. MRS FORBES'S BEDROOM. NIGHT

MRS FORBES *is half dressed, bent over a chair, reading a newspaper.* NUTTALL *stands behind her, still in his butcher's clothes. He is adjusting the wardrobe mirror.*

MRS FORBES: Poor Mr Metcalf. I didn't think he'd go to prison. You didn't tell me he'd go to prison.

NUTTALL: (*Taking down her knickers*) I don't care who goes to prison so long as it keeps your lodger off my back.

MRS FORBES: (*Looking at the paper again*) There's no fun in this for me, Douglas. It's all one-sided.

NUTTALL: You have a magnificent bum, Doris.

MRS FORBES: I don't like that word.

NUTTALL: Bottom, then.

MRS FORBES: That either.

NUTTALL: What then?

MRS FORBES: There isn't a word I do like. My husband never felt the need to refer to it.

NUTTALL: No news?

(MRS FORBES *shakes her head and reads an item from the newspaper on the Royal Wedding.*)

MRS FORBES: ". . . Currants, British Guiana. Demerara sugar, Barbados. Desiccated coconut, Ceylon."

NUTTALL: What's this?

MRS FORBES: The Empire. Who's sent what for the wedding cake.

NUTTALL: Look. Cheek to cheek to cheek.
  (*She looks round. He has his cheek against her bum and is looking in the wardrobe mirror.*)
MRS FORBES: Oh, Douglas, you are common. Why can't you just get on with it?
NUTTALL: I wish I had this on the slicer. I could sell it fifteen times over.
MRS FORBES: Be sharp. I've Mr Wormold's dinner to get.
  (NUTTALL *leans over* MRS FORBES.)
NUTTALL: Doris. When you go in, drop him a hint about Barraclough.
MRS FORBES: I'm fed up doing your dirty work, Douglas.
NUTTALL: Go on.
MRS FORBES: No. No.
  (MRS FORBES *looks pained and then a slight spasm crosses her face, indicating that* NUTTALL *is getting on with it. She waits with the patience of an animal.*)

35. INT. MRS FORBES'S DINING ROOM. NIGHT
A bare room. WORMOLD, *having just finished his thin chop and two veg., is holding the remains of his chop up to the light when* MRS FORBES *comes in with her tray.*
WORMOLD: Isn't that green?
MRS FORBES: (*Bringing her eye by* WORMOLD'*s*) Yes. It's spinach. You had spinach.
WORMOLD: So I did.
MRS FORBES: Did you enjoy it?
WORMOLD: I don't enjoy food, Mrs Forbes. I have no sense of taste, no sense of smell. I had German measles as a child.
MRS FORBES: A little more, Mr Wormold?
WORMOLD: There is no more, Mrs Forbes. I have eaten my ration.
MRS FORBES: We're only human, Mr Wormold.
WORMOLD: My experience has been, Mrs Forbes, that when people say they're only human it is because they have been

making beasts of themselves. (*Pause.*) Do you make a beast of yourself, Mrs Forbes?

MRS FORBES: My husband is missing in Malaya, Mr Wormold. I live the life of a widow.

WORMOLD: I hope so, Mrs Forbes. (*Folding his napkin with meticulous care*) I hope so.

(*She puts his plate on her tray.*)

MRS FORBES: I'll get your sweet.

(MRS FORBES *seems to linger.*)

WORMOLD: Yes, Mrs Forbes?

MRS FORBES: (*Reluctantly*) I was talking to a woman who gets her meat from Mr Barraclough. She says she gets some lovely stuff, only . . .

WORMOLD: Only what, Mrs Forbes?

MRS FORBES: Well, she's not always sure she's not eating something that's run in the 2.30. Know what I mean?

36. INT. MRS FORBES'S KITCHEN. NIGHT
His ear cocked, NUTTALL *is biting the last of the meat off his chop.* MRS FORBES *comes in and, putting her tray on the sink, reaches for something underneath it.*

MRS FORBES: (*Whispered*) I want this out of the house. Keep it somewhere else.

NUTTALL: Why?

MRS FORBES: He trusts me.

(MRS FORBES *pulls a tightly rolled, dark-stained, brown smock from under the sink. As she holds it out to* NUTTALL, *it unravels from her hand, dumping Nuttall's killing tackle on the floor. They freeze . . . the well-used knives, pig sticker, steel and hammer, on the floor between them.*)

37. EXT. BARRACLOUGH'S BUTCHER'S SHOP. DAY
There is a queue outside, in which we notice JOYCE *and* MOTHER, *almost in the door.* MRS FORBES *is at its head.* WOMEN *are coming out with parcels, smiling and happy. Suddenly*

the queue is hushed as WORMOLD *is seen to drive slowly by. Once he has gone on around the corner, they chatter expectantly again.*

38. INT./EXT. WORMOLD'S CAR/BACK STREET. DAY
Sitting with the window down, WORMOLD *watches* MRS FORBES *in the rear-view mirror, as she comes round the corner from Barraclough's. As she comes up she quickly hands her parcel to him through the window.*
MRS FORBES: They shaved women's heads for this in France.
    (*She walks on and doesn't look back.* WORMOLD *opens the parcel in his lap. The steak is very red and fleshy.*)

39. INT. BARRACLOUGH'S SHOP. DAY

JOYCE *and* MOTHER *have reached the counter.* JOYCE *is taking her three ration books from her handbag.*

JOYCE: I was registered with Mr Metcalf only he's had to close.

BARRACLOUGH: (*Winking*) I heard. Pork in the wardrobe. What would you like?

JOYCE: (*Hardly able to believe her ears*) What would we like, Mother? Steak?

(MOTHER *nods eagerly.*)

BARRACLOUGH: Certainly. (*Lifting a large flank of steak on to the counter, he proceeds to cut them a thick juicy slice.*) All right?

(JOYCE *and* MOTHER *cannot believe their luck. Parcelling*

41

up the steak, BARRACLOUGH *pushes it to them across the counter. Then suddenly* WORMOLD *strides into the shop, his parcel open in his hand.*)

WORMOLD: Right. That's it. Cease trading. Would you all kindly leave the premises.

JOYCE: Why?

WORMOLD: Horse, madam. Horse.

JOYCE: *Horse!*

(JOYCE *is horrified. Not so* MOTHER.)

MOTHER: I don't mind.

WORMOLD: Out, everybody. Out.

(WORMOLD *is shoving them out, when* MOTHER *slips past and tries to take their parcel off the counter.*)

Touch that, madam, and you're an accessory.

JOYCE: She's 74. Horse!

(*As chaos grows,* JOYCE *pushes* MOTHER *out through the mêlée.*)

40. INT. BARRACLOUGH'S SHOP. DAY

WORMOLD *and* BARRACLOUGH, *both somewhat white-faced, are alone in the shop, the doors of which are now locked. Outside, pressing their faces against the windows, are the angry* HOUSEWIVES. *They are in a very ugly mood, shouting and banging on the glass.*

The HOUSEWIVES *break a window.* WORMOLD *rattles the phone up and down, trying to get a line. He sighs and drops it back on to its cradle as he sees the police car draw up, and* INSPECTOR NOBLE *and* PC PENNY *get out.*

41. INT. BARRACLOUGH'S SHOP. DAY

Once in, INSPECTOR NOBLE *and* PC PENNY *experience the same fear of the angry, shouting* CROWD *banging and pressing against the glass.*

WORMOLD: (*Definitively*) It's horsemeat!

BARRACLOUGH: They eat it in Belgium.

WORMOLD: We're not in Belgium.

BARRACLOUGH: They ate rats in Stalingrad.

(*They prepare to force their way out.*)

INSPECTOR NOBLE: (*Looking accusingly at* WORMOLD) These used to be ordinary decent people.

(*They begin to force their way to the police car.*)

42. INT. ALLARDYCE'S OFFICE. DAY

Standing at the window with a cup of coffee ALLARDYCE *is watching* GILBERT *on the Parade below.* GILBERT *is standing in the middle of the road, waving his arms about. Finishing his coffee,* ALLARDYCE *glances at his watch, then takes his coat from the stand and puts it on.*

Slightly surreptitiously he takes a parcel wrapped in newspaper and puts it in his attaché case. Then, taking his empty coffee cup with a biscuit in the saucer he goes into the outer office.

His secretary DOROTHY *is sitting there, also watching* GILBERT. ALLARDYCE *puts his cup and saucer down.*

ALLARDYCE: Should the telephone ring, Dorothy, I've gone to see a client.

(*He is going out.*)

DOROTHY: Mr Allardyce.

(ALLARDYCE *stops.*)

Are you not eating this ginger nut?

(ALLARDYCE *shakes his head. He goes out and closes the door.* DOROTHY *has just taken the ginger nut and is about to dunk it in her coffee when the door opens.*)

ALLARDYCE: On second thoughts.

(*He takes the biscuit from her nerveless fingers and goes out again, leaving her bemused. Turning back to the window, she looks down at* GILBERT *waving his arms in the road.* ALLARDYCE *is seen to come up by* GILBERT'S *side.*)

43. EXT. THE PARADE. DAY

GILBERT *is directing the* PAINTER *in his premises. The* PAINTER *is standing in the window holding up the porcelain foot.*

43

To ALLARDYCE'S *casual glance the foot looks part of some much larger leg, going up into the shop.*

ALLARDYCE: (*A friendly greeting*) Mr Chivers.

GILBERT: (*Turning*) Chivers. Do you think I've got it (*meaning the foot*) in the right place?

ALLARDYCE: (*Meaning the premises*) Oh yes. Yes. Best place in town.

(GILBERT *turns, not understanding, but* ALLARDYCE *has gone.*)

44. EXT. NUTTALL'S SHOP. DAY

As ERNEST *pushes the blinds in for half-day closing, he tells every passer-by that "We're closed."* NUTTALL *can be seen in the shop, alone except for* MR LOCKWOOD.

45. INT. NUTTALL'S SHOP. DAY

NUTTALL *has just pushed a parcel wrapped in newspaper over the counter to* LOCKWOOD.

LOCKWOOD: Sad about Metcalf. You'll be the only butcher left soon.

(NUTTALL *disembowels a chicken.*)

We're all going to have to watch our step.

(NUTTALL *chops the head off the chicken.*)

NUTTALL: (*Holding his hand out for the parcel*) Mr Lockwood.

(LOCKWOOD *frowns and gives him the parcel.* NUTTALL *puts the chicken's head and giblets in it and gives it back to* LOCKWOOD, *who puts the parcel in his attaché case. He barges his way out past* ERNEST *coming in with the blind hook.* GILBERT, *passing on his bike, pulls up when he sees* LOCKWOOD.)

46. EXT. NUTTALL'S SHOP. DAY

GILBERT: Morning, Mr Lockwood. My lease ready to sign?

LOCKWOOD: (*As he walks on*) In due course.

GILBERT: (*Following with his bike*) No difficulty, is there?

LOCKWOOD: Yes. Time. It's in short supply.

(*Left in the road,* GILBERT *looks around awkwardly and then remounts his bike and pedals off.*)

47. EXT. STREET. DAY
GILBERT *is on his rounds again, cycling cheerfully along. Further up the street* DR SWABY *is on the point of leaving a patient's house. A* WOMAN *is holding the door and behind her we see an elderly lady* (MRS BEEVERS).

DR SWABY: (*To* WOMAN) I think you're doing the right thing. I'll send somebody round for her tomorrow. Tell her she's going to Bridlington. The grounds are immaculate. She'll be very happy.
(DR SWABY *raises his hand in a wave and then takes his leave going towards his car parked in the road.*)

WOMAN: (*Running*) Doctor. Doctor Swaby.

(DR SWABY *looks from his car to see the* WOMAN *running down the path towards him, waving a parcel in gaily decorated paper at him.* GILBERT *approaching on his bike has also seen the* WOMAN. DR SWABY *opens his car door into* GILBERT's *path, causing him to swerve and fall off.*)

GILBERT: Look out, you! Oh sorry, Dr Swaby.

(*A wagon coming the other way narrowly misses* GILBERT *sprawling in the roadway. The* WOMAN *throws her hands up in horror. The parcel flies into the air. Coming down it hits the roof of the car and bursts, flinging its contents over* DR SWABY. *Collecting himself,* GILBERT *looks up to find a seething* DR SWABY *gathering potato peelings and kitchen waste from the road and his person. Glaring at* GILBERT, DR SWABY *wraps this garbage in the remains of the gaily decorated paper. Showing no recognition of his having been at fault,* DR SWABY *then gets back into his car with his parcel and drives off leaving* GILBERT *sitting in the road.*)

48. EXT. BOWLING GREEN. AFTERNOON

ALLARDYCE *and* LOCKWOOD *are sitting by the pavilion, watching the game, attaché cases on their knees.* LOCKWOOD *looks at his watch.*

ALLARDYCE: I've never committed a crime before.

LOCKWOOD: I thought you were an accountant.

ALLARDYCE: (*Opening his case*) I've fetched her another ginger biscuit. Last week's went down so well.

(DR SWABY *arrives.*)

DR SWABY: Ready?

LOCKWOOD: Ready? We're ready.

(*They follow* DR SWABY *away, all with their little attaché cases.*)

DR SWABY: I had a little contretemps with that new chiropodist. Why we need chiropodists I don't know. Something wrong with their feet people can come to me. They'd always find a sympathetic hearing.

ALLARDYCE: You've got bacon rind on your shoulder.
  (DR SWABY *dashes the rind from his shoulder and violently
  wings it away. As they reach Dr Swaby's car they stop short.*
  GILBERT *is labouring up the road leading past the bowling
  green on his bike. He smiles at them and snatches a quick
  wave as he passes.*)

49. EXT. OPEN COUNTRY. AFTERNOON
GILBERT *pedals on up the narrow twisting moorland road. Dr
Swaby's car makes no allowance for him when it roars past, its
three occupants staring out disapprovingly.*

50. EXT. SUTCLIFFS' FARMYARD. AFTERNOON
ALLARDYCE, LOCKWOOD *and* DR SWABY *pick their way
across the mucky farmyard in their unsuitable shoes.* PRESTON, *the
loutish son of the farm stares at them.* MRS SUTCLIFF *comes out
of the house.*
  *The three visitors pick their way over to a long shed. Through the
open door we can see that it is lined with pig stalls, with a centre
aisle down the middle.* SUTCLIFF, *a rough-looking character, is
working at the far end.*
ALLARDYCE: We've come to see our friend.
  (*He waves his case.* SUTCLIFF *comes out of the shed.*)
SUTCLIFF: You want to watch out, coming all together. I'm
  the one who'll cop it.
DR SWABY: Nonsense, Sutcliff. (*Raises his attaché case*) I've
  come to examine your good lady.
LOCKWOOD: I'm here to draw up your will.
  (*They both look at* ALLARDYCE.)
DR SWABY: What are you here for?
  (ALLARDYCE *looks baffled.*)
ALLARDYCE: How do you mean?
  (DR SWABY *and* LOCKWOOD *exchange pitying looks and
  then open their attaché cases and take out their parcels.*
  ALLARDYCE *takes out his and begins to open it.* PRESTON
  collects the parcels and, taking ALLARDYCE's *from him, he*

47

*goes over to another open shed where he throws the complete
parcels into the hopper of a large mincer. Kicking a small
yapping dog out of the way,* PRESTON *then switches it on.*)
What about the paper?

SUTCLIFF: She eats the paper. She'd eat you.

ALLARDYCE: No.

(ALLARDYCE *looks to the others for reassurance, which is not
forthcoming. Leaving* PRESTON *with the mincer,* SUTCLIFF
leads them away out of the yard towards a wood.)

51. INT. DARK STY. AFTERNOON
It's pitch black. As SUTCLIFF *and the* OTHERS *are heard
approaching a* PIG *begins to grunt excitedly in the dark. The door
opens. As the light comes in we see that the "sty" is an old van.*

ALLARDYCE: Betty! Betty! Where's my Betty?
(*The* PIG *snuffles.*)
Hello, how's my friend? It's your Uncle Henry.

LOCKWOOD: (*Critically*) Not much fatter, and it's a bit since
we've been.

SUTCLIFF: She's put on a couple of stone, only she's gone
lame.

ALLARDYCE: Lame? Oh dear. Oh Betty.

DR SWABY: What's she doing, going lame?

SUTCLIFF: I don't know.

DR SWABY: You should know, the money we pay. Get the vet.

SUTCLIFF: Get the vet. You're barmy. This is an unlicensed
pig.

DR SWABY: Square him, Sutcliff. We pay you enough. Lame.
(SUTCLIFF *becomes uneasy.*)

ALLARDYCE: Here's something for your poorly foot, Betty. A
ginger nut, yes. You like ginger nuts.

52. EXT. "STY" WOODS. AFTERNOON
*The old van that is the "sty", sits without its wheels in a small
clearing in the woods.* LOCKWOOD, DR SWABY *and* SUTCLIFF
come out of the back of the van and DR SWABY *gives* SUTCLIFF

an envelope. ALLARDYCE *then comes out closing the door behind him and they walk back towards the farm.*

ALLARDYCE: I shall miss her, you know, when it comes to the point.

LOCKWOOD: Well, it's coming to the point.

53. EXT. NARROW BANKED ROAD. AFTERNOON
GILBERT *is labouring up the road. He is about to turn off the road down a track leading to Sutcliffs' farm, when Dr Swaby's car comes out unexpectedly, nearly fetching him off his bike, the third time that day.*

DR SWABY: (*Out of the car window*) Clown!

54. INT./EXT. DR SWABY'S BAR/MOORLAND ROAD.
AFTERNOON
DR SWABY *roars ahead, glaring back at* GILBERT *in his rear-view mirror.*

ALLARDYCE: (*In the back*) I see he's opening a surgery.

DR SWABY: You don't call a fly-blown room where you cut toenails a surgery. Where?

ALLARDYCE: On the Parade. Frank rented him it.

DR SWABY: This is a stab in the back.

LOCKWOOD: I didn't think.

DR SWABY: You're going to have to think. You're going to have to think of a way of getting him out.

ALLARDYCE: Why?

DR SWABY: (*Sweetly*) I don't like him.

55. EXT. SUTCLIFFS' FARMYARD. AFTERNOON
Squatting by the bucket as the mincer riddles into it, PRESTON *looks up as* GILBERT *arrives in the yard.*

PRESTON: Who's this?

SUTCLIFF: Her foot feller.

  (*They watch* GILBERT *dismount.*)

  Go fetch that lame bugger.

(*As* PRESTON *goes off,* SUTCLIFF *watches* GILBERT *go into the house.*)

56. INT. SUTCLIFFS' KITCHEN. AFTERNOON
Close up of big hands with a small knife, paring some skin on a foot.
GILBERT: (*To himself*) Touch of tinea pedis here.
    (MRS SUTCLIFF *looks.*)
    Athlete's foot.
MRS SUTCLIFF: Oh, do women get that?
GILBERT: Nothing to worry about.
MRS SUTCLIFF: I hear you were there when the Gestapo
    arrived.
GILBERT: Gestapo?

MR SUTCLIFF: (*Having come up silently behind* GILBERT)
Wormold.
(MRS SUTCLIFF *cries out in pain as* GILBERT *jumps.*)
GILBERT: Sorry. He made me jump.
MRS SUTCLIFF: You made him jump, you great puzzock.
SUTCLIFF: Have you got a minute?
(GILBERT *looks a bit askance but* SUTCLIFF *jerks his head authoritatively so he gets up.*)
MRS SUTCLIFF: He's not done me yet. Bernard. *Bernard.*
Bloody hell!

57. INT./EXT. LONG SHED/SUTCLIFF'S FARMYARD.
AFTERNOON
GILBERT, SUTCLIFF *and* PRESTON *are in one of the stalls in the shed. In the other stalls, pigs are stood up watching.*
   PRESTON *and* SUTCLIFF *are trying to corner the* PIG *for* GILBERT. *In the struggle* GILBERT *gets very mucky. Eventually they corner* BETTY *and hold her while* GILBERT *looks at her poorly foot.*
GILBERT: (*Holding up a nail*) Here's the culprit.
   (*He shows it to the* PIG, *which nuzzles him gratefully. A telephone is heard ringing.*)

58. EXT. SUTCLIFFS' FARMYARD. AFTERNOON
Suddenly MRS SUTCLIFF *runs out of the farmhouse, one shoe on, one shoe off and runs across to the long shed.*
   We hold on the farmyard as GILBERT *is hurried out of the long shed and into the farmhouse by* MRS SUTCLIFF. *Once* GILBERT *is out of the way,* SUTCLIFF *and* PRESTON *come out of the long shed with the* PIG *and herd it towards and into a dog kennel and shove a board over the opening. A moment later, Wormold's black car noses into the yard.*

59. INT. SUTCLIFFS' KITCHEN. AFTERNOON
MRS SUTCLIFF *rushes out of the pantry with a bowl of eggs.*
Putting them in a coal scuttle she then gets out a leg of ham which

she puts behind a cushion. GILBERT, *trying to clean his trousers, is a bit unsettled by all this. Finished,* MRS SUTCLIFF *sits down for* GILBERT *to go on with her feet.*

GILBERT: They're only old trousers.

MRS SUTCLIFF: Act normally.

GILBERT: I think you've trod in something.

(*Sighing at his fussing, she goes over to the sink and hoiks her leg up into the sink and runs the tap over her bare foot. Through the window she sees* WORMOLD *getting out of his car.*)

60. EXT. SUTCLIFFS' FARMYARD. AFTERNOON

WORMOLD *crosses the yard. The little dog is yapping at its kennel. Seeing* WORMOLD *it comes up affectionately to him whereupon* PRESTON *kicks it away.* SUTCLIFF *and* PRESTON *proceed to follow* WORMOLD *about.*

SUTCLIFF: Sometimes I wonder what the last war was for.

(WORMOLD *looks in the long shed, down the centre aisle and at the pigs stood up in their stalls, looking at him.*)

WORMOLD: The people, Mr Sutcliff. That was what it was for. Fair shares for all.

(*They leave the shed and cross the yard and go into the farmhouse.*)

61. INT. SUTCLIFFS' KITCHEN. AFTERNOON

MRS SUTCLIFF *hands* WORMOLD *a sheaf of forms.*

MRS SUTCLIFF: Sty specifications. Swill schedule. Slaughtering certificates.

SUTCLIFF: You find one wrong pig on this farm and I'll give you a hundred pounds.

WORMOLD: (*Unimpressed*) If I do it'll cost you more than that.

(WORMOLD *looks hard at* GILBERT.)

I've seen you before.

GILBERT: How do you do.

WORMOLD: Yes. You were there the other day.

(*He walks over to* GILBERT *and looks down at his case of*

instruments, he picks up one of the sharp knives and studies it.
He looks at GILBERT.)
You get about.

GILBERT: I do people's feet.
(WORMOLD *looks at his soiled trousers.*)
I knelt in something.

WORMOLD: Maybe you ought to have a look at my feet. Can you fit me in?
(GILBERT *opens his appointment book and gives him a card.*)

GILBERT: Tuesday at 4?
(WORMOLD *takes the card and pauses at the door, surveying the farmyard.*)

WORMOLD: On we go. No rest for the wicked.
(*He sets off across the yard towards his car. The little dog is yapping at his kennel.* WORMOLD *stops and looks over. He glances at the farmhouse and then goes over to the kennel.* SUTCLIFF *and* PRESTON *exchange anxious glances. Crouching down by the kennel,* WORMOLD *gives the little dog an affectionate pat and a stroke. He then leaves. As he drives off,* PRESTON *goes out to the kennel.* GILBERT *is picking up his newspaper to tip the bits of toenail, hard skin, etc., on to the fire.*)

SUTCLIFF: Is that skin? Put it in the pig bucket. It's a delicacy.
(GILBERT *tips it into the bucket.*)
You want to save any scraps. Peelings and whatnot. All contributions gratefully received. And we'll see you all right. How much do we owe you?

GILBERT: Five shillings.

SUTCLIFF: Soon earned. Sharper than farming.
(*He peels one off a vast roll of notes. As* GILBERT *searches for change* SUTCLIFF *is drawn to the kitchen table.*)
Where's the ham?

MRS SUTCLIFF: Oh, pissing hell!
(*She goes and gets the ham from behind the cushion, rubs it on her apron and bangs it down on the dish.*)

SUTCLIFF: What's happened to the fire?
(*He picks up the coal scuttle and without looking at the contents swings it at the fire, covering it with three dozen eggs.*)
You silly cow, Hilda!

62. INT. CHILVERS' GARAGE. DAY
JOYCE *and* MOTHER *are sitting in the back seat of the pre-war Vauxhall Big Six. We do not see* GILBERT.
JOYCE: Where shall it be today, Mother? Any preference?
MOTHER: Where what?

JOYCE: Our destination. I thought we might have a little run to Harrogate.

(*The car is gently rocked.*)

MOTHER: Joyce.

JOYCE: What, Mother?

MOTHER: We're in the garage.

JOYCE: I have to breathe, Mother. I have to breathe.

(*We see* GILBERT *cleaning the car.*)

MOTHER: Why doesn't he put the wheels on, Joyce?

JOYCE: (*Winding down the window*) Because we've no coupons, Mother. Gilbert can't get the juice. I've got a husband who can't get the juice. What are you eating, Mother?

MOTHER: A cream cracker.

JOYCE: Where did you find it?

MOTHER: In my cardigan.

JOYCE: Well, get out of the car and eat it. You know the rules. No crumbs in the car.

(MOTHER *get out.*)

MOTHER: He's missed a bit here, Joyce.

(JOYCE, *still in the car, looks out of the open window at the bit* MOTHER *is pointing at.*)

JOYCE: You've missed a bit here, Gilbert.

(*As* GILBERT *comes from the back of the car, with his polishing rag,* JOYCE *gets out and we see it's on blocks.*)

GILBERT: I never have. I can see my face in that.

JOYCE (*Sadly*) So can I.

63. EXT. NUTTALL'S SHOP. DAY

A long queue stretches along the front of the shop and beyond. MRS ALLARDYCE *and* VERONICA, *and* MRS SUTCLIFF *are just inside the shop.* JOYCE *is a little way behind them, stood outside with a* STONY-FACED WOMAN *between her and them.*

There is a poster of Princess Elizabeth and Lieutenant Mountbatten in Broadbent's window and next door the MAN *is hanging up Union Jack bunting.*

JOYCE *is trying to get herself noticed, but is being obstructed by the* STONY-FACED WOMAN *ahead of her in the queue.*

MRS SUTCLIFF: Who's this woman behind me?

MRS ALLARDYCE: (*Surveying queue but not stopping talking*) Busy this morning, of course it will be now the other two are closed down, the chiropodist's wife.

JOYCE: Veronica's making great strides.

MRS ALLARDYCE: Really?

JOYCE: How're you going on with "The Soldier's Chorus", Veronica? Keeping the fingers bent?

(VERONICA *looks as if she would like to keep her fingers bent round* JOYCE'*s throat.*)

(*Nailing* MRS SUTCLIFF) Gilbert was telling me you'd like us to save some of our scraps for your pigs.

MRS SUTCLIFF: Well . . . yes . . . if you've got anything to spare.

MRS ALLARDYCE: (*Over-sweetly*) But don't give them anything you can eat yourself.

(NUTTALL *comes over and puts a "Closed for Lunch" notice in the window. Then he forces the door closed.* JOYCE *is left outside.*)

NUTTALL: Sorry. I'm run off my feet.

(VERONICA, *inside the shop, pulls a face at* JOYCE *outside.*)

64. INT. GILBERT'S PREMISES. DAY

The PAINTER *and his* BOY *are having their lunch, sitting on boxes. As* JOYCE *looks in,* GILBERT *picks up his framed diploma and holds it up in the place he has chosen for it.*

JOYCE: You ought to put up a brass plate.

GILBERT: Brass? (*Laying down his diploma*) Bakelite would do to be going on with.

JOYCE: Bakelite?

(JOYCE *becomes aware of a flat, dour voice. The* PAINTER'*S* BOY *is reading the newspaper out loud for the* PAINTER. *It is an article on the royal wedding cake.*)

PAINTER'S BOY: ". . . raised garlands of York roses mingle

56

with the daintiness of ears of corn, happy symbol of plenty, then twine upwards to join with sprays of orange blossom in the centre medallion."

JOYCE: Is this the wedding dress?

PAINTER'S BOY: No. It's the cake.

65. INT. CHILVERS' KITCHEN. DAY

GILBERT *is cutting the leaves off some rhubarb. He puts them into a parcel of waste, potato peelings, apple peelings, etc., that he is preparing for Sutcliff's pigs.* JOYCE, *followed by* MOTHER, *comes*

*in carrying the dirty breakfast dishes to the sink. She goes to scrape
the bits into the bin.*

GILBERT: (*Stopping her*) Here. Here. It's for the pigs.

(JOYCE *gives his somewhat sparse collection a critical look.
Opening a tin of corned beef, she puts half in the parcel. She
then opens a tin of cling peaches and dumps that in the
parcel.*)

JOYCE: "Don't give them anything you can eat yourself."

(GILBERT *and* MOTHER *look on wonderingly.*)

I'm not having her thinking we just put rubbish in the
bin. I wish I'd one or two maraschino cherries, then it'd
show we had cocktails.

GILBERT: We don't have cocktails.

JOYCE: (*Sighing*) I'm carrying you, Gilbert.

66. INT./EXT. "STY"/WOODS. DAY

ALLARDYCE *is inside the back of the old van leaning over the
stall. He is looking at the* PIG, *which is smiling and grunting away
and snuffling at* ALLARDYCE's *hands and pockets.* ALLARDYCE
scratches its back.

ALLARDYCE: Now, then, Betty. Have you missed me? How's
your foot? Is it better? It's better, isn't it? You're
champion again, aren't you? What is it? What is it, Betty?

67. EXT. NARROW BANKED ROAD. DAY

GILBERT *is labouring up the road towards the track down to
Sutcliffs' farm*

68. EXT. SUTCLIFFS' FARMYARD. DAY

DR SWABY *sits fuming in his car waiting for* ALLARDYCE.
SUTCLIFF *is by his window trying to make conversation.*
ALLARDYCE *runs into the yard from the woods, opens the
passenger door and takes out a brown-paper parcel.*

ALLARDYCE: I forgot to give Betty these. She looked right
downcast.

(DR SWABY *looks contemptuous.* ALLARDYCE *nips round*

58

the car and gives the parcel to SUTCLIFF, *who proceeds to open it.*)

There's a ginger nut in there, she likes them whole so could . . .

(SUTCLIFF *is watching* GILBERT *cycle into the yard.*)

SUTCLIFF: I don't like him seeing you here.

(*As* GILBERT *goes and knocks on the door, he sees* SUTCLIFF *pass a brown-paper parcel to* ALLARDYCE. *Guiltily,* ALLARDYCE *pops the parcel through* DR SWABY'S *open window.*)

ALLARDYCE: You think he might tipple to it?

(*Having been opened, the parcel's contents of kitchen waste tips out all over* DR SWABY'S *lap.*)

DR SWABY: (*Tight-lipped and furious*) Get in.

(DR SWABY, *brushing off his lap, watches* GILBERT *waiting at the farmhouse door.*)

Jaunty toenail clipping little sod. Biking around.

(*Seeing* DR SWABY *looking at him,* GILBERT *touches his hat.*)

Don't touch your hat to me, you festering, bunion-scraping little pillock. I want him out of that shop.

ALLARDYCE: (*Seating himself uneasily by* DR SWABY) Frank's got the lease back now. It's in his office.

DR SWABY: (*Psychopathically calm and sweet again*) Well, what are we waiting for then, Henry?

(GILBERT *goes into the farmhouse.*)

69. INT. SUTCLIFFS' KITCHEN. DAY

MRS SUTCLIFF: Now let's see if I can find you a little something.

(GILBERT *waits awkwardly as she goes into the larder.*)

(*Out of vision*) Leg of ham suit you?

(*In the larder,* MRS SUTCLIFF *picks up a ragged shank of ham with a bit of meat on it. She sniffs it.* MRS SUTCLIFF *comes out of the larder with what looks to be a substantial brown-paper parcel which she ties with string.*)

Keep this under your hat.

(GILBERT *gives what he imagines is a sophisticated wink, feeling he's joined the club.*)

70. EXT. SUTCLIFFS' FARMYARD. DAY

GILBERT *waves goodbye to* MRS SUTCLIFF, *who comes out of the house and goes into an open shed with Gilbert's parcel. Screaming,* PRESTON *rushes out of the open shed with a spade raised above his head.* GILBERT *sees the rat just as* PRESTON *smashes it with the spade. Picking it up by its tail,* PRESTON *watches* GILBERT *start off up the track and then returns to the open shed.*

71. INT. OPEN SHED. DAY

MRS SUTCLIFF *has emptied Gilbert's parcel into the hopper of the mincer and is looking at the contents contemptuously. We see the rhubarb leaves. Then the dead rat is flung on top.* PRESTON *starts the motor and the stuff starts riddling through the mincer, potato peelings, blood, leaves and rat, dropping into the bucket below.*

72. EXT. NARROW BANKED ROAD. DAY

GILBERT *has stopped to pump up a tyre. Hearing a noise, he looks up over the bank. In glimpses he can see* PRESTON *going through the woods with a bucket.*

73. EXT. "STY"/WOODS. AFTERNOON

As PRESTON *opens the back door we follow him in. The* PIG *looks up at him expectantly.*

PRESTON: Soon you're going to die, pig.

(*The* PIG *smiles.*)

I'm going to kill you, pig.

(*The* PIG *smiles on.*)

That'll wipe the smile off your face.

74. EXT. NARROW BANKED ROAD. DAY

As PRESTON *disappears towards the farmyard,* GILBERT *is seen*

*cautiously threading his way through the woods and up to the old
van in the clearing.*

75. EXT./INT. WOODS/"STY". DAY
GILBERT *opens the van's back door and sees the* PIG *contentedly
feeding on the terrible contents of the bucket. Seeing* GILBERT, *the*
PIG *recognizes him and moves towards him excitedly. Failing to
recognize the* PIG *from their earlier encounter,* GILBERT *stumbles
back down the steps and shuts the door as he thinks the* PIG *is
trying to escape.*

76. EXT. ARCADIA CINEMA. DAY
MOTHER *and* JOYCE *come out and walk off down the Parade.*

77. EXT. TOWN. DAY

MOTHER *and* JOYCE *bump into* GILBERT.

GILBERT: We're in.

JOYCE: In where?

GILBERT: (*Handing her the parcel*) Ham. We've joined the club. We're on the circuit.

MOTHER: Ham?

GILBERT: Have a look.

JOYCE: In the street? I will not.

GILBERT: This is just the beginning. Listen, why don't we splash out? I've just got to call at the surgery, you go to the Grand and order afternoon tea. (*Turning*) You'd like that, wouldn't you, Mother?

(MOTHER *looks at* JOYCE, *fearful of what this courtesy portends.*)

78. EXT. THE PARADE. DAY

Full of joy, GILBERT *walks towards his premises. He says a cheery first-name hello to the* CHEMIST, *who is stood out at his door. The* CHEMIST *is reticent, his attention on something further down the Parade. Several of the other* PROPRIETORS *are seen to be looking out, down the Parade.*

GILBERT *notices the* PAINTER'S BOY *coming past on his bike.* GILBERT *calls to him cheerily. The* BOY *ignores him.*

Outside Gilbert's premises parked back to back are the painter's handcart and Dr Swaby's car. The PAINTER *comes out of the shop, carrying some of his gear to his cart. Seeing his porcelain foot and other paraphernalia piled on the pavement,* GILBERT *parks his bike at the kerb in front of Dr Swaby's car and picks up the foot and carries it back to the surgery.*

GILBERT: (*To* PAINTER) No. All this has to stay put.

(*The* PAINTER *seems not to have heard him and locks the surgery premises.*)

No, don't do that. I'll lock up. Have you finished? You haven't finished.

(GILBERT *is becoming confused.*)

62

LOCKWOOD: (*Out of vision*) I have to ask you for the keys to these premises.

(GILBERT *turns to find* LOCKWOOD *peering at him, sitting in the car with* DR SWABY *at the wheel. The* PAINTER *has given* LOCKWOOD *his keys and is going to his cart.*)

GILBERT: (*Showing them*) Keys? I've got keys.

(GILBERT *is lost.*)

LOCKWOOD: I know. (*Leans across* DR SWABY *and snatches them through the window.*) I want them.

GILBERT: Here.

(*He puts his porcelain foot on the bonnet.*)

DR SWABY: He's put his foot on my bonnet.

LOCKWOOD: You're in breach of agreement. Failure to declare a change of use.

ALLARDYCE: (*In the back*) You're supposed to declare a change of use.

DR SWABY: Take your foot off my bonnet.

(DR SWABY *is closing the window.*)

GILBERT: You knew. You knew what I wanted it for.

LOCKWOOD: You need planning permission.

ALLARDYCE: You could apply for planning permission.

GILBERT: Who should I apply to?

DR SWABY: Me.

(DR SWABY *starts up the car and* GILBERT *hurriedly snatches his foot off the bonnet as the car suddenly moves off, running over his bicycle as it does so.* GILBERT *is aghast, and we see* ALLARDYCE's *anguished face looking back at him and his shattered bike as the car speeds off. In anger and frustration* GILBERT *kicks the pile of painters' rubbish. Paint goes all over his trouser bottoms.*)

79. INT. HOTEL TEA LOUNGE. AFTERNOON

A ladies orchestra is playing. In the background we see decorations being put up for the Royal Wedding Dinner. Photographs of the royal couple. Bunting. Flowers. Gilt chairs being carried through. These preparations intrude on JOYCE *and* MOTHER *who are having tea.*

JOYCE: You see this is where I belong, Mother. Get me into a long dress and surround me with sophisticated people, I'd bloom. (*Pats the parcel, sitting on Gilbert's waiting chair.*) This is just the beginning.

(MOTHER *takes an interest in the parcel and starts to unwrap it. The* HOTEL MANAGER *takes note. He begins to hover.*) Ham, eggs, stuff under the counter. It'll come, you see.

MOTHER: (*Seeing the parcel's contents*) It's a bit of scrag end.

(MOTHER *starts to pick at it.*)

HOTEL MANAGER: Excuse me, Madam. Patrons are not permitted to consume their own food on the premises.

(JOYCE *is deeply humiliated. At which point* GILBERT

*staggers in and threads his way through the tables with his pot
foot, his paraphernalia and his paint-stained trousers.*)

JOYCE: Gilbert. Are you deliberately trying to humiliate me?

GILBERT: I've got something that will humiliate you more.

(*The orchestra strikes up, drowning their conversation but we
see* JOYCE *hear* GILBERT's *bad news.*)

JOYCE: This town. These people. They're going to have to be
made to sit up and take notice. They're going to have to
be made to realize who we are. My father had a chain of
dry cleaners. We regularly used to drink wine with the
meal as Mother well knows. Telling us what we can and
can't do. My father wore a carnation in his buttonhole
every day of his life. Lend me threepence.

(GILBERT *gives her a threepenny bit which she pushes
towards the unimpressed* WAITRESS *as a tip.* JOYCE *leading,
they begin to thread their way out.*)

I want a future that will live up to my past. Only when's it going to start? That's what I want to know.

MOTHER: (*Stopping by a table*) These are having cream cakes.

80. INT. HOTEL LOBBY. DAY
On their way out, JOYCE and MOTHER spot the menu for the Royal Wedding Dinner, which is posted in the lobby.

JOYCE: (*Reading out the menu*) Melon surprise. Moules niçoise. Porc royale. . . It breaks your heart.

GILBERT: Listen, I've had just about enough. If you want roast pork we can have roast pork. We can have it next Sunday if you want it. And the Sunday after that. And the Monday. And the Tuesday. We can have pork till you're blue in the face. You could be fed up of pork. Porc royale! (*Tears down the menu and turns to MOTHER.*) And you. You can have bacon, ham, sausage, pork pies. Tripe. Pig's feet. Liver. Kidneys. You can pig yourself on pork if you want. Come on.

JOYCE: Take no notice, Mother. He's just out to torment you.

GILBERT: I mean it. We could. We can.

JOYCE: How? How?

(*GILBERT is already starting to regret what he's said.*)

GILBERT: Steal a pig.

(*A DELIVERY BOY struggles in with more decorations for the Royal Wedding Dinner.*)

JOYCE: What did you say?

GILBERT: Nothing, let's go.

JOYCE: Steal a pig?

(*They make their way out against yet more decorations coming in.*)

81. INT. CHILVERS' SITTING ROOM. AFTERNOON
JOYCE is taking another pupil, MERVIN, through his faltering exercises. MOTHER is sitting cracking nuts, an activity JOYCE finds distracting.

JOYCE: You've dropped a bit, Mother.

(A banging starts elsewhere in the house and a pained expression crosses JOYCE's *face. Life is not as she would like it to be.)*

82. INT. CHILVERS' HALL. AFTERNOON

VERONICA *is watching* GILBERT *redecorate the spare room, which he is having to make into his "surgery". Putting down the hammer he takes up his paint brush again.* JOYCE *lets* MERVIN *out of the living room and he goes to the door.*

JOYCE: Haven't we forgotten something, Mervin?

MERVIN: Oh sorry, Miss.

JOYCE: Mrs.

(Opening his hand, he gives JOYCE *her five shillings fee. She looks pained and humiliated. He then leaves.)*

Go on in and start your piece, Veronica.

*(*VERONICA *sullenly complies, regarding* MOTHER *eating her nuts with distaste. As the familiar piece begins* JOYCE *finds herself looking in the mirror in the spare room.)*

Good job I put my foot down about children.

*(*GILBERT *is puzzled.)*

GILBERT: Why bring that up?

JOYCE: Well, we wouldn't have had the room, would we?

(The look on GILBERT's *face makes it plain he would have preferred children to the room.)*

(Contemptuously) Steal a pig! It's not as if there are pigs to steal. If there were pigs to steal butchers would be stealing them.

*(*GILBERT *says nothing.)*

It's you all over. All talk. Promises. You were going to take this town, Gilbert.

GILBERT: Listen. This morning I went up to Sutcliffs' farm.

*(*VERONICA *stops playing.* GILBERT *looks up sharply. His manner gives* JOYCE *cause for thought.)*

JOYCE: *(Calling) Da capo*, Veronica. And a little more *mezzo forte.*

(As JOYCE *closes the door lest they be overheard* GILBERT

starts telling JOYCE *what he has seen in the woods by Sutcliffs' farm.*)

83. INT. GILBERT'S AND JOYCE'S BEDROOM. NIGHT
GILBERT *lies in bed, watching* JOYCE *at her dressing table.*
GILBERT: It's all a bit clandestine for me, Joyce.
JOYCE: Whose pig is it?
GILBERT: I don't know. It'll belong to them at the farm.
(JOYCE *goes into the bathroom where we see her preparing her contraceptive device, an antiquated douche with a rubber tube.* GILBERT *is unable to see these preparations.*)
(*To himself*) I wish I hadn't mentioned it. (*Shouting to* JOYCE) It's illegal.
JOYCE: (*Shouting from bathroom*) It wouldn't be illegal. Why is it illegal? A black-market pig's illegal.
GILBERT: I wish I'd never mentioned it. Anyway, we've no means of transport.
JOYCE: We've got the car.
GILBERT: It's on blocks.
JOYCE: Get it off the blocks.
GILBERT: And put a pig in it? "No crumbs in the car, Gilbert." "No cake on the seat." A pig in the car!
JOYCE: I could put a paper down. This is an emergency.
GILBERT: Let's sleep on it.
(JOYCE *brings the douche into the bedroom.*)
GILBERT: (*Alarmed*) What's put this into your head all of a sudden? Tomorrow's a working day.

84. INT. "STY". DAY
The PIG *is lying in its stall, not very well.* DR SWABY, LOCKWOOD *and* ALLARDYCE *are looking at her anxiously. The* PIG *farts.*

85. EXT. SUTCLIFFS' FARMYARD. DAY
SUTCLIFF, PRESTON *and* NUTTALL *are coming out of the farmhouse and making for the "sty".*
NUTTALL: (*To* PRESTON) Do you know how to do it.

68

PRESTON: I've done it before.

SUTCLIFF: And a right mess you made of it.

PRESTON: I want to be there.

SUTCLIFF: You can watch. Only it's not going to be stuck today. We'll have to wait till it's better. Them rats wouldn't have upset it, would they, Preston?

PRESTON: No. It's had rats before.

SUTCLIFF: It's what I say. Rhubarb leaves always mean the squits. You should know that, Preston.

86. INT./EXT. "STY"/WOODS. DAY

SUTCLIFF, PRESTON *and* NUTTALL *crowd into the back of the old van, with* ALLARDYCE, DR SWABY *and* LOCKWOOD.

SUTCLIFF: Rhubarb leaves.

PRESTON: I knew it wasn't the rats.

ALLARDYCE: Rats! You've never been giving her rats?

SUTCLIFF: No. *Scraps.*

ALLARDYCE: Could you not give her something, Charles? You're the doctor.

DR SWABY: Thank you. This is a pig not a person. You want a vet.

ALLARDYCE: The principle must be the same.

DR SWABY: How would you know?

LOCKWOOD: Take a bit of weight off her. Diarrhoea always does.

DR SWABY: Oh, are you a doctor now?

LOCKWOOD: I am not a doctor, Charles, but my wife has two topics of conversation. One is the royal family and the other is her bowels.

(*The* PIG *farts again and they stagger back at the sheer horror of the stench.*)

PRESTON: Why not kill it now?

ALLARDYCE: No.

NUTTALL: I'm not having this joker in my fridge a minute longer than I have to. I've fetched up my tackle. I'll kill it in a day or two.

DR SWABY: The dinner's on Thursday.

SUTCLIFF: I still haven't had my invite.

DR SWABY: Blame Henry.

SUTCLIFF: I'm taking such a risk.

DR SWABY: (*Giving him an envelope*) Not for much longer.

ALLARDYCE: There! She's stood up.

87. INT. CHILVERS' GARAGE. EVENING

GILBERT *is putting the wheels back on his car. While* MOTHER *squats by a rear wheel with a kerosene lamp,* GILBERT *is straining to tighten a nut. There are newspapers on the back seat and* JOYCE *can be seen intermittently through the far window as she pumps up the other rear tyre with a hand pump.* GILBERT *stumbles as he moves to the back of the garage.*

GILBERT: Over here.

> (MOTHER, *still crouched at the rear wheel, comes over with the torch to help* GILBERT, *who ferrets out a can of petrol that he has hidden.*)

This was going to take us to Scarborough.

JOYCE: (*As she pumps up the tyre*) Scarborough! It'll take us further than Scarborough. It'll take us to the top in this town will this. They'll be lining up, wanting to get to know us then. Dr Swaby. Mr Allardyce. Oh yes. And I'll give them cocktails and we'll nibble at those refined little sausages before going in to a sumptuous meal. It's not just pork. It's power.

GILBERT: (*Pouring the petrol in*) Leave off, Joyce.

MOTHER: Sausage. Have you been having sausage?

GILBERT: (*Crossly*) Hold it up.

JOYCE: She used to be such a grand woman.

88. INT. MRS FORBES'S HALL. NIGHT

MRS FORBES *is listening at a door. She knocks and goes in.*

MRS FORBES: Mr Wormold, what are you doing, sitting in the dark? (*Switches the light on.*) Put the fire on.

WORMOLD: We've been asked to save power.

(She collects a tea cup and a side plate.)

MRS FORBES: You are a model, Mr Wormold. Will Mr
Barraclough go to prison?
(There is a silence.)
I wouldn't do it for anybody else.

WORMOLD: You believe in my mission, Mrs Forbes. No news
of Mr Forbes?

MRS FORBES: No, Mr Wormold. *(Crouches down by his chair
and puts the fire on.)* Stop in tonight.

WORMOLD: I must catch the killer. The man who butchers
the pigs.

MRS FORBES: He doesn't have to be a butcher?

WORMOLD: Who knows?
*(WORMOLD shakes his head. MRS FORBES is not getting
up.)*
What?

MRS FORBES: You've not been crying?

89. INT. CHILVERS' KITCHEN. NIGHT

GILBERT *is getting ready to go out.* JOYCE *is holding some
newspapers.* MOTHER *can be seen asleep in the sitting room.*

GILBERT: *(Indicating MOTHER)* You'd better get her out of
the way.
(JOYCE goes to her and shakes her.)

JOYCE: Wake up, Mother. It's time you were in bed.
*(GILBERT is putting together a parcel of tasty scraps. Coming
in, MOTHER tries to pinch one. It is JOYCE who stops her.)*
No, Mother. Naughty.
(She slaps her hand. MOTHER frowns.)
Goodbye. Good luck.
*(She kisses GILBERT passionately. He isn't so keen on the
kissing as she is and is groping behind him for his torch.)*

MOTHER: When did you start all this kissing?
*(GILBERT takes the torch and goes out the back door. JOYCE
runs to the door.)*

JOYCE: *(Whispered)* Gilbert.

GILBERT: (*Out of vision*) What?

JOYCE: I hope it's a clean one.

(*She then takes the newspapers and considers where to put them. She wanders out of the kitchen. We follow her into the hall and into Gilbert's newly decorated "surgery". Having considered it for a moment she starts to put the newspapers down on the floor.*)

MOTHER: (*In doorway*) Is the sweep coming?

90. INT. SUTCLIFFS' SITTING ROOM. NIGHT

They are sat round, very torpid, listening expressionlessly to the radio. A comedy programme. Gales of laughter from the radio. None from the SUTCLIFFS. SUTCLIFF *gets up and winds the clock.*

SUTCLIFF: Did you ought to go see how that pig is going on, Preston?

(PRESTON *doesn't make an immediate move.*)

MRS SUTCLIFF: I miss the war.

(*Pause.*)

SUTCLIFF: Come on, Preston. You reckon to be i/c pig.

(PRESTON *slowly begins to get himself together.*)

91. INT./EXT. "STY"/WOODS. NIGHT

GILBERT *comes up the steps and through the back door, into the old van.*

GILBERT: Hello, Sunshine. Hello, Pig. Pooh, you stink, pig.

(*He is shining the light of the torch on the* PIG. *He pulls up the front of the stall. The* PIG *watches this and snuffles.*)

We're going to go for a little walk.

(*Sensing the scraps in the parcel, the* PIG *comes forward out of the stall grunting.*)

Shsh. Here, here.

(GILBERT *stumbles down out of the back of the van throwing down scraps for the* PIG, *who gobbles them up. Gracefully the* PIG *comes down the steps. Out of her sty, the* PIG *sniffs the air and looks as if she is going to wander. To* GILBERT'S

72

relief the PIG *finds another scrap and snuffles it up. She begins to thread her way through the trees after* GILBERT's *trail of scraps.*)

92. INT. SUTCLIFFS' KITCHEN. NIGHT
PRESTON *comes through from the sitting room. He becomes furtive and shuts the door behind him. He gets out Nuttall's killing tackle. Taking the pig sticker, he puts his boots on and then, collecting a torch, goes out leaving the door open.*

93. EXT. NARROW BANKED ROAD. NIGHT
GILBERT *is panicking. The* PIG *is standing on the top of the bank, eating scraps from* GILBERT's *hand but refusing to come down for the pile of scraps* GILBERT *has on the back seat of his car. A torch flashes in the woods.* PRESTON *is going to the "sty".* GILBERT *gets into the car, he's off. The* PIG *sniffs the air. She turns her head looking back, watching* PRESTON. *Snuffling, the* PIG *comes down the bank and climbs into the back of the car.* GILBERT *reaches out and shuts the door as he lets his handbrake off and rolls away.*

94. INT. SUTCLIFFS' KITCHEN. NIGHT
The door is open. The cold is coming in.
SUTCLIFF: (*Out of vision*) Preston! Preston!
    (SUTCLIFF *is seen as he crossly opens the sitting-room door.* MRS SUTCLIFF *is seen sitting beyond him.*)
MRS SUTCLIFF: I don't wonder he failed the sea scouts.
    (SUTCLIFF *goes to close the kitchen door, when* PRESTON *bursts in. He flings the pig sticker down on the table where it sticks quivering.* SUTCLIFF *looks at him in wild surmise.*)
That's my table.

95. INT./EXT. GILBERT'S CAR/OPEN COUNTRY. NIGHT
GILBERT *still has the hill with him and is rolling down without the engine. The* PIG *is sitting on the back seat, very much enjoying the ride. The mood is triumphant.*

96. INT. GILBERT'S SURGERY. NIGHT

JOYCE *sits staring.* GILBERT *also staring. They are almost mesmerized.*

JOYCE: It's off its paper. Gilbert. It's off its paper.

GILBERT: It won't know to stay on it.

JOYCE: Fetch some more papers then.

> (GILBERT *goes, still watching the* PIG. *It looks cheerfully back at him.*)
> (*Calling, panic-stricken*) Gilbert! Quick. It's doing its business.
> (GILBERT *returns and watches the* PIG, *which we do not see, with distaste.*)

GILBERT: It'll be nervous.

> (*Catches a whiff of the smell.*) Jesus!
> (*He opens the door. She shuts it.*)

JOYCE: I don't want her next door smelling it.

> (*They stare at it again.* JOYCE *puts a cloth to her face.*)
> I can't stand this. You'd better do it now.

GILBERT: Do what?

JOYCE: Kill it. Look at the floor.

GILBERT: My nice clean surgery. I'd imagined it in the kitchen.

JOYCE: I hadn't.

GILBERT: I keep wanting to call it something. A name.

JOYCE: Why? You're going to kill it, Gilbert. You're going to slit its throat.

GILBERT: Couldn't you get fond of it?

JOYCE: I couldn't, wetting all up and down.

GILBERT: Your mother does.

JOYCE: I didn't hear that, Gilbert. I can't stand this. Look at the floor. I was quite right not to want kiddies if this is what it's like. Kill it, Gilbert.

GILBERT: I've never killed anything in my life.

JOYCE: You should've thought of that.

GILBERT: Whose idea was it?

JOYCE: Yours. Who did you think was going to kill it?

GILBERT: I thought I could ask somebody.

JOYCE: Ask somebody? Ask somebody? This is a crime.

GILBERT: What do I do it with?

JOYCE: One of your feet knives. They're precision tools.

GILBERT: Not for pigs.

JOYCE: It's got hard skin. I thought you were an expert when it came to hard skin.

(GILBERT *shakes his head and goes up to the* PIG. *It nuzzles his shoes.*)

Listen, Gilbert Chilvers, this country has just emerged from a second world war, a war in which millions of people died, most of them killed by their fellow men.

GILBERT: Not with chiropodist's tools.

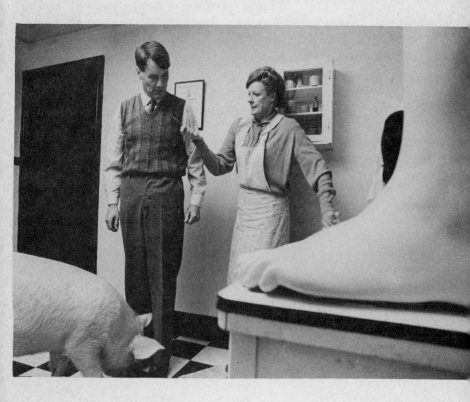

JOYCE: It's not the tools. It's the will. It's doing its business again. Trust you to pick one with diarrhoea.

GILBERT: A strange place. Strange people. You can understand it. We ought to let it settle down.

JOYCE: Settle down? *Kill it.*
(*She thrusts a knife into his hand and goes out.* GILBERT *strokes the* PIG.)

GILBERT: With this? (*It is a very small knife.*) How?

97. INT. CHILVERS' LANDING. NIGHT
JOYCE *is spraying scent about from an old-fashioned scent spray.*
MOTHER *appears in her nightie.*

MOTHER: Joyce.

JOYCE: What?

MOTHER: Can you smell a smell? I can smell a smell.

JOYCE: (*Continuing to squirt*) There's no smell, Mother. You're imagining it.

MOTHER: I wondered if it was me.
(GILBERT *comes upstairs.*)

GILBERT: I can't do it.

MOTHER: (*As* GILBERT *passes*) It's him. He smells, Joyce.

JOYCE: He doesn't smell, Mother. Go to bed.
(MOTHER *goes to bed, unconvinced.*)

MOTHER: He does smell, Joyce.
(*Something is knocked over downstairs.*)

98. INT. CHILVERS' HALL. NIGHT
JOYCE *and* GILBERT *come quickly down the stairs. They find the surgery door ajar.*

JOYCE: Oh my God.
(*There is a noise. They look to the sitting room. The door is ajar.*)

99. INT. CHILVERS' SITTING ROOM. NIGHT
JOYCE *and* GILBERT *appear in the doorway, watching aghast. The* PIG *is eating fruit out of a bowl on the dining-room table.*

JOYCE: That bowl was a wedding present.

GILBERT: It's not to know that.

(*The* PIG *runs into the kitchen, followed by* GILBERT.)

100. INT. CHILVERS' KITCHEN. NIGHT

GILBERT *shuts the door carefully. Then* JOYCE *opens it a fraction and slips through with a cloth.*

JOYCE: Another parcel in the umbrella stand.

(JOYCE *goes to wring the cloth out in the sink. Her eye catches the gas oven.*)

Maybe we could put it to sleep.

(*She takes a bowl of food from the larder and puts it into the gas oven.*)

101. INT. MOTHER'S BEDROOM. NIGHT

MOTHER *sits on her bed. She sniffs the air. After a moment's thought she sniffs herself.*

102. INT. CHILVERS' SITTING ROOM. NIGHT

GILBERT *and* JOYCE *are waiting outside the kitchen door. We see the crack beneath the door has been stuffed up.* JOYCE *listens at the door.*

MOTHER: (*Out of vision*) Joyce.

JOYCE: What?

MOTHER: (*Out of vision*) I think it's gas.

JOYCE: No.

MOTHER: (*Out of vision*) I can smell gas.

GILBERT: Go to bed.

JOYCE: It's past your bed time.

(*Suddenly there is a ring at the front door.*)

103. INT. CHILVERS' HALL. NIGHT

MOTHER, *standing at the top of the stairs, watches* JOYCE *go to the door.* JOYCE *seems unaware of* MOTHER.

MRS TURNBULL: Mr Turnbull thought he could smell gas.

JOYCE: (*Nodding*) It's Mother. She switched it on and never lit it. She's getting like that.

MRS TURNBULL: So long as we know.

(*She is going away but turns back and tries to peer round the door.*)

You can't smell something besides? I don't know. A bit of a sickly smell.

(JOYCE *nods, closing the door.*)

JOYCE: It's Mother again. She had a bit of a do with her tummy. She keeps bringing stuff back.

(MRS TURNBULL *spies* MOTHER's *feet at the top of the stairs and crouches down to see her.*)

MRS TURNBULL: Bless her.

(JOYCE *closes the door, her face like an axe.* GILBERT *is looking through to her from the kitchen door on the far side of the sitting room.*)

JOYCE: Did it go off?

(*As if in answer the* PIG *pokes its cheerful head round the kitchen door. Seeing* JOYCE, *it makes towards her.* JOYCE

violently indicates MOTHER's *presence to* GILBERT.
GILBERT *turns the gas off, vaults the furniture and just beats the* PIG *to the hall, shutting it in the sitting room and out of* MOTHER's *sight.* JOYCE *sits on the steps in despair.*)
Could we poison it?
GILBERT: If we poison it we can't eat it.
(*In thought,* GILBERT *looks up.* MOTHER *hovers on the landing.*)
(*Looking down to* JOYCE) We're going to have to take professional advice.
MOTHER: What about? Me? Joyce.
JOYCE: What?
MOTHER: Don't go calling Dr Swaby. He'll put me away.
JOYCE: We're going to have to tell her.
(GILBERT *makes a gesture of despair.*)
Come down, Mother.
MOTHER: You just told me to go to bed.
JOYCE: Come down.
MOTHER: I can still smell that smell.
JOYCE: Never mind the smell, Mother. Sit down.
MOTHER: Are you sure it's not me?
JOYCE: No, Mother, love, it's not you.
(GILBERT *listens to the sitting-room door.*)
Mother. Love. I've got something to tell you. We've got a pig in the house.
(*Not sure her daughter isn't being sarcastic,* MOTHER's *gaze flickers to* GILBERT. MOTHER *says nothing.*)
Do you understand, Mother? A pig.
(MOTHER *looks at* GILBERT *again, fearfully.*)
MOTHER: What sort of a pig?
JOYCE: A pig, Mother. A proper pig.
(MOTHER *is silent.*)
MOTHER: Do you want to put me in a home?
(GILBERT *gestures in despair.*)
JOYCE: Shut up.
GILBERT: I didn't say anything.

(MOTHER *begins to cry*.)

MOTHER: Dr Swaby put Mrs Beevers away. He asked her the name of the prime minister, she didn't know and they carted her off to Low Moor. You want my room?

GILBERT: We don't want your room. Why does saying we've got a pig in the house mean we want your room?

JOYCE: (*Crisply*) Leave this to me, please, Gilbert. This is my mother. It's not like Mrs Beevers, love. Mrs Beevers imagined things. That's why Dr Swaby sent her away. You don't imagine things. It's just that we've got a pig in the house.

GILBERT: It's so's if you catch a glimpse of it you won't think you're going bananas. (*Muttering to* JOYCE) Though she is going bananas.

JOYCE: (*Hissing*) She wouldn't think she was going bananas, love, if you pulled your socks up and cut its throat.

MOTHER: What's this bananas? I could eat a banana.

GILBERT: There are no bananas. There is a pig. There are no bananas.

JOYCE: Gilbert! Love, forget the bananas. There aren't any bananas, but there is a pig.

GILBERT: Only tell her if anybody comes round there isn't a pig.

JOYCE: Yes, that's right, love. If anybody should call, there isn't a pig. With us, a pig. Anybody else, no pig.

MOTHER: Who's going to come? Is it Dr Swaby? He came to Mrs Beevers.

JOYCE: Nobody's going to come, Dr Swaby, nobody. But if anybody does come, no pig.

MOTHER: He told her she was going to Bridlington. She ended up in Low Moor. It was her house.

JOYCE: Nobody is going to put you in Low Moor, Dr Swaby or anybody. We love you, Mother. We wouldn't put you away. It's just we're in the slightly unusual situation where there is a pig in the house.

GILBERT: Show her it.

JOYCE: I won't show her it. She's 74, and it's past her bedtime. Go to bed, love. With luck – (*Looks meaningfully at* GILBERT) – in the morning all this will seem like a bad dream.
(MOTHER *goes slowly upstairs, accompanied by* JOYCE, GILBERT *peers in through the sitting-room door. He grimaces. Below, the* PIG *thrusts its snout out. It shoulders aside* GILBERT *and the door and comes out heading for the stairs.* GILBERT *heads it off, shepherds it into the surgery and shuts it in.*)

104. INT. CHILVERS' LANDING. NIGHT
GILBERT, *ready for bed in his dressing gown, tries the bedroom door. It's locked.*
GILBERT: Joyce. Joyce.
JOYCE: (*Out of vision*) Have you done it?
(GILBERT *goes downstairs.*)

105. INT. GILBERT'S SURGERY. NIGHT
GILBERT *sits in his dressing gown with the smiling* PIG.

106. INT. HOTEL FUNCTION ROOM. AFTERNOON
ALLARDYCE: Betty. Betty. Betty.
LOCKWOOD: We're going to look that silly.
DR SWABY: Silly? We're finished.
LOCKWOOD: We've put a lot of money into that pig, Howard.
INSPECTOR NOBLE: It's my understanding it doesn't exist.
DR SWABY: You'll wish it existed on Thursday, when you're sitting down to a scrutty bit of lettuce and tomato.
INSPECTOR NOBLE: Why can't he slaughter one of his other pigs?
DR SWABY: Because the other pigs are all licensed and listed, stupid!
INSPECTOR NOBLE: Steady, Charles, I'm still a police officer.
LOCKWOOD: You're not behaving like one.
INSPECTOR NOBLE: I'll sniff around.

LOCKWOOD: Sniff around. It'll be the other side of the
Pennines by now, sold to the Jewboys in Manchester.
INSPECTOR NOBLE: Pork?
DR SWABY: Pork, nylons, anything. I don't know what the
last war was about.

107. INT. GILBERT'S SURGERY. AFTERNOON
In an open book, we see stark photographs of cuts, joints of pork. The
PIG *sits pleasantly, watching* JOYCE *and* GILBERT *study the book.*
JOYCE: (*Toying with large knife*) How to kill them, that's what
we want. Does it say?
GILBERT: It doesn't say.
JOYCE: Let me look.
(*As* JOYCE *flicks through the book,* GILBERT *glances at the*
PIG. *It catches and returns his look warmly.*)
It doesn't say. You'll just have to improvise.
(*She puts the knife in his hand. A loud knock at the front door*
startles them. GILBERT *attempts to hide the large knife on his*
person while JOYCE *quickly gathers up the book.*)

108. EXT. CHILVERS' FRONT DOOR. AFTERNOON
VERONICA *has arrived for her piano lesson. As she waits for the*
door to be opened WORMOLD *comes up, with his attaché case. The*
door is opened by MOTHER. *She looks from one to the other.*
MOTHER: No pig. No pig.
(MOTHER *looks again at the man with the attaché case. Has*
he come to commit her? She cowers back. JOYCE, *then*
GILBERT *appear anxiously behind her.*)
JOYCE: Come in, Veronica. (*Mouthing to* WORMOLD) She's 74.
GILBERT: (*Behind* JOYCE *and* MOTHER) Come in, Mr
Wormold.

109. INT. CHILVERS' SITTING ROOM. AFTERNOON
VERONICA *is doing her piece, with* JOYCE *standing, partially*
blocking our view, at the end of the piano.
VERONICA: Your house smells. Our house doesn't smell. Poor
people smell.

(JOYCE *looks back over her shoulder to* WORMOLD, *who is sitting in an armchair having his feet done.*)
JOYCE: It's Mother. She's getting a bit careless.
WORMOLD: I can't smell anything. But then I can't smell anything. German measles.
GILBERT: You have perfect feet. I don't know why you come.
(WORMOLD *looks round, looks at Gilbert's knives, but says nothing.*)

110. INT. CHILVERS' HALL. AFTERNOON
MOTHER *listens at the sitting-room door, which is open a crack.*
MOTHER: No pig.
(*There is a grunt behind her from the surgery. She sneaks a look in. The* PIG *gets out, crosses the hall and goes into the sitting room.* MOTHER *follows it.*)

111. INT. CHILVERS' SITTING ROOM. AFTERNOON
MOTHER: No pig.
(*They look up at her. Seemingly unnoticed, the* PIG *wanders through.*)
VERONICA: There's a pig! There's a pig!
(*Looking to* VERONICA, WORMOLD *is about to see the* PIG *that is passing behind his chair.* GILBERT *sticks his knife into* WORMOLD's *foot.*)
GILBERT: Sorry.
(*The* PIG *disappears into the kitchen.* MOTHER *follows.*)
VERONICA: A pig!
JOYCE: Pigs here? Don't be silly. The idea!
(*A rigid hand on* VERONICA's *shoulder forces her back to the keyboard.*)
Da capo, Veronica. Come on, *da capo*.
(*It has been a narrow squeak.*)

112. INT. CHILVERS' LANDING. EVENING
MOTHER *is standing thoughtfully, with her hand on the knob of her bedroom door. She opens it and looks in. The* PIG *is sitting on*

her eiderdown looking out of the window. The front door bangs
downstairs. MOTHER *and the* PIG *look out and watch*
WORMOLD *going away down the path. Then he stops and looks*
back.

113. INT. CHILVERS' HALL. EVENING

GILBERT: Do you think he noticed anything?

> (*There is a ring at the doorbell.* GILBERT *opens the door.*
> WORMOLD *stands there.*)

WORMOLD: Thought so.

> (GILBERT *and* JOYCE *don't move.* WORMOLD *steps in,*
> *takes his attaché case from the hall stand, waves it and leaves.*
> JOYCE *shuts the door.*)

GILBERT: There must be easier ways of getting roast pork
than this.

> (*At the top of the stairs,* MOTHER *and the* PIG *look out from*
> *her bedroom.*)

JOYCE: It's got beyond roast pork now, Gilbert. It's
self-respect.

GILBERT: Joyce.

JOYCE: Our marriage is in a corner. I want to push down the
walls. Open out. Take your clothes off.

GILBERT: (*Startled*) What?

JOYCE: There'll be blood. Strip.

> (*She helps him strip down to his underpants and socks.*
> GILBERT *occasionally murmuring in protest.*)

GILBERT: But she's my friend.

JOYCE: Kill her. (*Puts the large knife in his hand*) Kill your
friend.

> (*She pushes him upstairs.* MOTHER *and the* PIG *disappear*
> *into her bedroom.* GILBERT *goes in after them. The* PIG *runs*
> *out.* GILBERT *follows. They come down the stairs.* JOYCE
> *heads them into the surgery. Grabbing* GILBERT, *she kisses*
> *him deeply.*)

Do it for me.

> (*Pushing him into the surgery she closes the door behind him.*)

87

114. INT. GILBERT'S SURGERY. EVENING
GILBERT *advances on the* PIG *with the large knife in one hand
and now a small knife in the other. The* PIG *gives him a look of
pure love.*

115. INT. CHILVERS' HALL. EVENING
JOYCE *waits, listening and breathing hard. Suddenly terrific
scuffling and screaming is heard from the surgery. Then quiet. The
door opens slowly.*
GILBERT: (*Shattered and bloody*) Joyce.
JOYCE: Oh my darling.
GILBERT: I've cut my finger.
> (*The* PIG, *still very much alive, pushes its head round the
> door.* JOYCE *thrusts* GILBERT *away.*)
JOYCE: Coward! Yellow! You're yellow, Gilbert Chilvers.
GILBERT: Joyce.
JOYCE: A pathetic cringing nancy. Don't touch me . . . nancy!
> (GILBERT *is dressing.*)
> Where are you going?
GILBERT: For a drink. I'm going to have a drink, then I'll be
able to do it.
JOYCE: You won't, I should have married a man.
GILBERT: I will. I promise.
JOYCE: Nancy!
> (GILBERT *rushes out.* JOYCE *looks at the* PIG, *then
> purposefully puts on an apron. She gets the knife and begins to
> move in on the* PIG.)

116. INT. HOTEL FUNCTION ROOM/KITCHEN. NIGHT
*The preparations for the Royal Wedding Dinner, which we
observed earlier, are now nearly complete. Three or four tables run
the length of the room, one running across the top. Floral
decorations are being prepared. Portraits of Princess Elizabeth and
Lieutenant Mountbatten being put into position. We track through
this to the kitchen. Where we find DR SWABY, LOCKWOOD,*

INSPECTOR NOBLE *and* NUTTALL *sitting around despondently, holding a council of war.*

LOCKWOOD: A hundred and fifty people. A hundred and fifty *people.*

(*He opens a bare cupboard.*)

INSPECTOR NOBLE: It'll be in the papers, of course. They'll jump on it. "Leading Lights in Dinner Fiasco."

(LOCKWOOD *opens another cupboard. The same.*)

DR SWABY: Of course it's practical Socialism. That's what it's going to be like now. What's yours is mine. Excuse me while I help myself. I'd have them bastinadoed. I'd flay them alive.

LOCKWOOD: What about some tinned salmon?

DR SWABY: Tinned salmon? Tinned salmon? I've got the North Western Area President of the Prudential Building Society coming. You don't offer Arthur Cunliffe tinned salmon.

INSPECTOR NOBLE: "Civic Row Over Paltry Fare."

NUTTALL: I've been trying to put my hands on a few chickens. (*Shakes his head.*) People I've dealt with for years.

DR SWABY: Well, I'm not surprised. Not surprised at all. God, it's a nasty piss-stained little country now is this. It's like this new Health Service. Do you realize that any little poorly pillock is henceforth going to be able to knock on my door and say, "I'm ill. Treat me." Anybody! Me!

(*The* HOTEL MANAGER *comes in.*)

HOTEL MANAGER: I can put my hands on two turkeys in Bradford.

LOCKWOOD: Two? *Two?* We've got a hundred and fifty people coming, and Jesus isn't one of them.

DR SWABY: Two turkeys in Bradford. Five years of war and that's what it's come to: two turkeys in Bradford.

HOTEL MANAGER: Well, do you want them or don't you? I've got him on the phone.

(NUTTALL, LOCKWOOD, DR SWABY *and* INSPECTOR

NOBLE *get up and go with the* HOTEL MANAGER. *They see*
GILBERT *sitting at the bar*.)
DR SWABY: We're finished, you and me, Lockwood. That's
what's coming to the top. The scum. No class. No
breeding. No morals.
INSPECTOR NOBLE: No pig.
DR SWABY: I give this country five years.

117. INT. ALLARDYCES' SITTING ROOM. NIGHT
VERONICA *can be heard practising her piece.* ALLARDYCE *sits in
his chair, very glum, the newspaper on his knee.* MRS
ALLARDYCE, *without speaking to him, removes the paper and
ostentatiously reads about tomorrow's royal wedding. The piano
stops.* VERONICA *comes in and sits on the arm of her mother's
chair. She regards poor* MR ALLARDYCE *with some hostility.*
VERONICA: It smells at piano.
MRS ALLARDYCE: Well, they don't have as much money as
we do.
VERONICA: They've got a pig.
MRS ALLARDYCE: (*Looking at* HENRY *dozing*) They're not the
only ones.
VERONICA: I saw it. Walking about the house
MRS ALLARDYCE: Don't tell stories, or you'll get a big nose.
Bedtime.
VERONICA: Shall I kiss Daddy?
MRS ALLARDYCE: Please yourself.
(VERONICA *decides she won't and goes out with* MRS
ALLARDYCE.)
VERONICA: (*Out of vision*) I did see a pig. It was all stinky.
(ALLARDYCE *is roused from his doze. He sits for a while,
thinking. Then gets up and goes to the foot of the stairs.*)
ALLARDYCE: (*Calling*) Veronica?

118. INT. CHILVERS' LANDING. NIGHT
JOYCE *is face to face with the* PIG. *She makes a grab for it. She
misses. It runs into the bathroom.*

MOTHER: Joyce. I want to use the toilet.

JOYCE: You can't. Go somewhere else.

MOTHER: Where?

JOYCE: Anywhere.

> (*She is cornering the* PIG *in the bathroom, but it knocks her aside and runs out.* JOYCE *rests exhausted.*)

MOTHER: Joyce. Why don't we leave him and the pig and just go to Grange over Sands and live?

JOYCE: It's too late for Grange over Sands, Mother.

> (*She begins to stalk the* PIG *again.*)

II9. INT. ALLARDYCES' DINING ROOM. NIGHT

MRS ALLARDYCE *sits waiting at the dinner table. Two plates set.*

Allardyce's plate is laden, but he is not there. MRS ALLARDYCE *sighs. Eyes the food.*

MRS ALLARDYCE: I'm waiting.

    (*Looking cross, she starts to help herself.* ALLARDYCE *enters, transformed. He is carrying a newspaper. He scrapes his dinner on to the paper. Then takes some of the contents of a tureen.*)

Henry!

    (*As an afterthought* ALLARDYCE *turns back and scrapes* MRS ALLARDYCE's *dinner on to the paper too. He wraps it all up and rushes out.*)

120. INT. HOTEL BAR. NIGHT

GILBERT *drinks in sad determination.*

121. EXT. HOTEL. NIGHT

ALLARDYCE *rushes into the hotel with his parcel. But someone is watching the hotel in a car. It is* WORMOLD.

122. INT. HOTEL BAR. NIGHT

GILBERT *is struggling with another drink. In the background,* ALLARDYCE *is seen to go into the function room.* GILBERT *gags on the drink he is forcing down. Recovering, he finds* INSPECTOR NOBLE *at his side, with* NUTTALL *at the other side.*

INSPECTOR NOBLE: Drink?

GILBERT: Me?

INSPECTOR NOBLE: My birthday this year.

GILBERT: No. I'm due back.

    (NUTTALL *sniffs* GILBERT's *clothes.* NOBLE *also does so.*)

INSPECTOR NOBLE: Been round the farms?

GILBERT: Farms?

INSPECTOR NOBLE: You smell a bit rustic.

NUTTALL: Pigs, I'd have said.

GILBERT: Got to go to the toilet.

    (*He gets up and goes towards the Gents.*)

123. INT. HOTEL GENTS. NIGHT

There are six stalls in the lavatory. The end one is occupied and as GILBERT *comes in we see the* MAN *glance at* GILBERT. *Suddenly* GILBERT *is conscious of someone on either side of him, also pissing. It is* INSPECTOR NOBLE *and* NUTTALL. *He doesn't say anything. Then* DR SWABY *comes in and stands in a stall and so does* LOCKWOOD. ALLARDYCE *tries to, but there is no room for him, so he hangs about behind. From his agitated demeanour he is plainly the only one who actually wants a piss.*

LOCKWOOD: How much do you want?

GILBERT: Beg pardon?

DR SWABY: You've got something we want. Something that belongs to us. Something with four legs and a little curly tail.

INSPECTOR NOBLE: Shall we adjourn?

(They are all leaving.)

ALLARDYCE: *(Stepping into a stall)* Hang on. I haven't been.
(ALLARDYCE *steps into a stall, thankful at last to be able to
relieve himself. But the* MAN *in the end stall now sidles up
and stands in the stall next to him. A look of consternation
comes over* ALLARDYCE's *face and he rapidly buttons up and
leaves, still not having managed to empty his bladder.)*

124. INT./EXT. WORMOLD'S CAR/HOTEL. NIGHT
WORMOLD *studies the men as they come out of the hotel. He
becomes agitated –* NUTTALL *is not among them. Then* NUTTALL
does come out. As he sets off in his van, WORMOLD *follows.*

125. INT. CHILVERS' HALL. NIGHT
GILBERT *opens the door.*
GILBERT: *(Going into sitting room)* Come in.
(*They follow him in,* MOTHER *watching them pass from
behind the door.)*
MOTHER: No pig. No pig.
(*Seeing* DR SWABY, MOTHER *claps her hands to her face in
horror.)*

126. INT. CHILVERS' SITTING ROOM. NIGHT
GILBERT: I'll just get my wife.
DR SWABY: We don't want your wife. We want the pig.
MOTHER: There is no pig. No pig.
(GILBERT *goes.*)
I know the name of the prime minister. I know what year
it is. I've been going to beetle drives till quite recently.

127. INT. JOYCE'S AND GILBERT'S BEDROOM. NIGHT
JOYCE, *knife in hand, is crouched by the dressing table.* GILBERT
comes in.
JOYCE: Don't move. I've got it cornered.
GILBERT: Stop. You can't.
JOYCE: Out of my way, *nancy!*

GILBERT: Dr Swaby's downstairs. Mr Lockwood.

JOYCE: Downstairs? But I'm not dressed.

GILBERT: It's their pig. We stole their pig.

JOYCE: (*Stunned, large knife in hand*) *Their* pig?

GILBERT: We stole their pig.

JOYCE: We? *You*. Get me my dress.

> (*The bedroom door is pushed open as we hear* ALLARDYCE's *voice.*)

ALLARDYCE: (*Out of vision*) (*Enticingly*) Betty. Who's this then, Betty?

> (*Round the door comes his hand holding a ginger nut biscuit.* JOYCE *can only stare. The* PIG *appears from behind the dressing table and makes a bee-line for the ginger nut.*)

128. INT. CHILVERS' SITTING ROOM. NIGHT

GILBERT: I wasn't to know.

INSPECTOR NOBLE: It was theft. Whoever it belonged to it was theft.

DR SWABY: You're a professional man. You've got letters after your name.

GILBERT: We were hungry.

LOCKWOOD: Hungry? People aren't hungry. Who's hungry? Who's your butcher?

> (NUTTALL *is peeping out through a crack in the curtains.*)

NUTTALL: I can't satisfy everybody.

> (ALLARDYCE *comes in. The* PIG *follows him.*)

ALLARDYCE: She's in very good condition. Did she have a bit of a tummy upset?

GILBERT: (*Wearily*) Yes.

INSPECTOR NOBLE: The important thing is the property has been recovered, the status quo has been restored. You are happy, the police are happy . . . it's all been a big mistake.

DR SWABY: Mistake! I want this man crucified.

> (INSPECTOR NOBLE *takes* DR SWABY *on one side.*)

INSPECTOR NOBLE: You crucify him, Wormold crucifies you.

LOCKWOOD: He's got us by the scrotum.

ALLARDYCE: Did she take to you? I found her very affectionate.

GILBERT: I did too.

DR SWABY: Henry! (*To* GILBERT) Listen, you tapeworm. You've been found out in a nasty, cheap little crime. I'd like to see you put away for a long time. I'd like to see you drummed out of whatever miserable association you chiropodists belong to and hounded out of this town with your tail between your legs. However, in Westminster Abbey tomorrow morning a young couple are getting married, of a purity and a nobility scum like you just can't comprehend. As a gesture to them we're going to say nothing about this, but take a tip from me. Leave this town. We don't want you. (*Turning to the others*) Now let's get the pig and get out of here.

NUTTALL: We can't. We're being watched.

(*At which point* JOYCE *comes in, looking like Greta Gynt, in her cocktail dress, with a corsage, a trolley of drinks and a tray of cocktail snacks.*)

JOYCE: Dr Swaby, Mr Lockwood, Mr Allardyce! And Inspector Noble. This is an unexpected pleasure. I gather there's been some silly, silly, misunderstanding over this . . . this animal. Well, we're all civilized people and I'm sure we can talk it over. Give Dr Swaby a cocktail snack, Mother.

(*She looks round for* MOTHER, *but she is not there.*)

Mother!

(*She goes out into the hall and finds* MOTHER *cowering there, terrified of* DR SWABY, *but still managing to eat the cocktail snacks.* JOYCE *propels her back into the sitting room.*)

Hand them round, Mother. (*Mouthing to the others*) Seventy-four, and never misses a trick.

(*While* MOTHER *offers round the snacks,* JOYCE *tries unsuccessfully to get them to have drinks.* MOTHER *has no more success with the cocktail snacks,* ALLARDYCE *being the*

*only one to take one, and he looks round in order to give it to
the* PIG. *To each one* MOTHER *is whispering "No pig. No
pig."*)

(*Nailing* ALLARDYCE) I think little Veronica is going to
startle us one of these days. I'm going to throw caution to
the winds and have a sweet sherry. Nobody else?
(*Awkward pause.*)

MOTHER: (*To* DR SWABY) I went by train to Lytham two
years ago to see my sister-in-law. I travelled all by myself
and I changed *twice*. Didn't I, Joyce?

JOYCE: Dr Swaby's not interested in your holidays, Mother.
Gilbert, I don't think we want that animal in here while
we're having our cocktails, do we?
(ALLARDYCE *is feeding the* PIG *cocktail snacks, those, at
any rate, that* MOTHER *isn't eating.*)

DR SWABY: Let's get the pig and go.

NUTTALL: (*Looking through curtains*) We can't. He's sat
outside.

INSPECTOR NOBLE: Who?

NUTTALL: Wormold. He suspects me.

INSPECTOR NOBLE: Jesus. Is there a back way?

JOYCE: Alas, no.

INSPECTOR NOBLE: Can you get over the wall?

LOCKWOOD: We can't get the pig over the wall.

INSPECTOR NOBLE: I'm not thinking about the pig. I'm
thinking about me.

DR SWABY: (*Barring the way*) We're all in this together.

INSPECTOR NOBLE: (*To* NUTTALL) Why should he suspect
you?

LOCKWOOD: Because he's the only flaming butcher left, that's
why. He's shopped all the others. Now it's his turn.

NUTTALL: (*Hurt*) That's unkind. There's only one thing to
do. I shall have to kill it here.

ALLARDYCE: Here?

GILBERT: Now?

JOYCE: Slaughter it here? What a splendid idea. We'd be only

too pleased. All our facilities are at your disposal.
(*She brings out the large knife.* NUTTALL *takes it
ponderously.* JOYCE *smiles a disarming smile.*)

NUTTALL: I'm going to need lots of hot water. And get
Preston round. Ring Sutcliff's.
(GILBERT *puts more coal on the fire.*)

MOTHER: (*To* DR SWABY) Seven nines are sixty-three.

129. INT. CHILVERS' HALL. NIGHT
ALLARDYCE *is saying his last farewells to the* PIG. *It's snuffling
cocktail snacks from his hand.* GILBERT *witnesses this scene as he
comes up from the cellar, below the stairs, with a heavy hammer.
He hides it behind his back.*

GILBERT: We could . . .

ALLARDYCE: What?

GILBERT: (*Looking about*) We could let her go.

ALLARDYCE: Yes? Where?

GILBERT: I don't know. Set her up somewhere in a sty. Not kill her, just keep her.

ALLARDYCE: They'd go mad. All right.

GILBERT: I've got a car. Grab hold.

(*As* GILBERT *moves towards the back kitchen door,* NUTTALL *comes out of the surgery.*)

Too late. (*Suddenly opening the door*) Go on, Betty, go on. (*Barging his way through,* NUTTALL *slams the door, locks it and takes the key. Turning, he looks at* GILBERT *and* ALLARDYCE.)

NUTTALL: Silly twats.

(*Grabbing the hammer off* GILBERT, *he goes back into the surgery, weighing the hammer in his hand. Assembled in there is an* ad hoc *killing tackle, mostly drawn from Joyce's kitchen.*)

130. INT. CHILVERS' SITTING ROOM. NIGHT

The back-boiler fire is roaring away. It is swelteringly hot. DR SWABY, LOCKWOOD *and* INSPECTOR NOBLE *sit there sweating while* JOYCE *makes desultory conversation.*

JOYCE: I must apologize for this room. It's in dire need of decorating. More sherry, Inspector?

INSPECTOR NOBLE: Don't mind if I do.

(DR SWABY *disgusted by him letting the side down, peeps through the curtains.*)

LOCKWOOD: I wonder what he thinks we're doing.

DR SWABY: Playing cards. It's a perfectly normal activity.

JOYCE: Bridge! Why didn't I think of it? Do you play, Doctor?

DR SWABY: No.

(LOCKWOOD *also shakes his head. Pause.* ALLARDYCE *comes in quietly. He is holding himself back.*)

JOYCE: The royal wedding is exciting a great deal of interest.

(*Pause.*)

DR SWABY: Could I ask you something?

JOYCE: Certainly.

DR SWABY: Have you ever had any mental illness?

(NUTTALL *pops his head round the door. He is wearing a floral apron, one of Joyce's.*)

NUTTALL: There might be some noise. Put the wireless on.

JOYCE: We don't need the wireless.

(*She approaches the piano.*)

131. INT. GILBERT'S SURGERY. NIGHT

GILBERT, *also wearing one of Joyce's floral aprons, is trying to hold the* PIG'S *head still.* JOYCE *is heard to start playing Ivor Novello's "Rose of England" on the piano.* NUTTALL *raises the heavy hammer.* GILBERT *cringes, waiting for the blow. There is a knock on the door.* NUTTALL *stops just short with his hammer. He jerks his head at* GILBERT.

132. INT. CHILVERS' HALL. NIGHT

The piano playing loudly in the sitting room, GILBERT *opens the door in his apron.*

PRESTON: (*Anxious*) Am I too late?

(NUTTALL *beckons him sharply but then sends him back for* GILBERT's *apron. As* PRESTON *puts it on,* NUTTALL *hustles him into the surgery and shuts the door. Left in the hall,* GILBERT *covers his ears and sits at the foot of the stairs.*)

133. INT. CHILVERS' SITTING ROOM. NIGHT

JOYCE *is playing with* élan. *She talks over her shoulder as she plays.*

JOYCE: Nice that he's in the Navy. Of course she was in the ATS, Princess Elizabeth. I believe she can drive a heavy goods vehicle. Not that she has to, of course. Still, nice to have something like that up your sleeve. Were you heavily involved in the war, Mr Lockwood?

(LOCKWOOD *loosens his collar, sweat pouring down his face.*)
Too modest to say, I know. Gilbert did his bit, in the ARP. I was in the St John's Ambulance. Lost count of the cups of tea I served. They also serve. I must say I'm looking forward to the wedding. I read in the paper they are going to spend the honeymoon at Broadlands.

DR SWABY: (*To* LOCKWOOD) Unfortunate name. Could be an institution.

JOYCE: Of course, it's what we do best, isn't it, the pageantry? The carriages passing through the streets, the Household Cavalry, the bells ringing out. Oh, England. It's like a fairy tale.
(*There is a shrill scream from the* PIG.)
I know they're going to be very happy.
(ALLARDYCE *bursts into tears.*)

134. INT. CHILVERS' HALL. NIGHT
GILBERT *is sunk against the banister in despair as* MOTHER *creeps anxiously down the stairs.* NUTTALL *comes out of the surgery with two brimming buckets of blood and* PRESTON *following.*

NUTTALL: Gangway.
(MOTHER *flattens herself against the wall, horrified.*)
The water hot?
(GILBERT *nods.* NUTTALL *starts up the stairs.*)
(*To* PRESTON) With a bit more leisure I'd make black pudding. (*To* GILBERT) Got a razor?

135. INT. CHILVERS' SITTING ROOM. NIGHT
GILBERT *comes in, he is plainly upset and puts his arm round* ALLARDYCE. *Through the open door can be seen the hindquarters of the dead* PIG.

GILBERT: I'm sorry.

DR SWABY: Sorry? I thought you called yourself a medical

man. The first requirement of a medical man is to have no
feelings.

(NUTTALL *comes in.*)

NUTTALL: I want a hand. We've got to get it upstairs.

DR SWABY: I'm dressed up.

LOCKWOOD: I have a hernia.

JOYCE: (*Brightly*) My brother-in-law has a hernia.

(ALLARDYCE *goes meekly out.* GILBERT *follows.*)
What a charming man. (*Knocks back the sherry.*) So
sensitive. I teach the daughter piano. One day I feel she
will surprise us all.

(*There is a sound of a great fart from the* PIG *as it is lifted up
the stairs.*)

136. INT. CHILVERS' HALL. NIGHT

MOTHER *stands looking up the stairs.* NUTTALL *comes down,
followed by* GILBERT *and* ALLARDYCE. *They go into the sitting
room.*

NUTTALL: Right, when I've seen to the carcass I'll leave.

INSPECTOR NOBLE: I leave first.

NUTTALL: I'm the one he's watching. I leave first but empty-
handed, right? You take the pig.

DR SWABY: We're not taking the pig.

NUTTALL: Do you want the pig, or don't you?

(MOTHER *comes in.*)

MOTHER: Joyce. Can I use the toilet?

JOYCE: Of course, Mother. There's no need to ask. (*Mouthing*)
Seventy-four.

MOTHER: (*Confidentially to* DR SWABY) Eleven elevens are a
hundred and . . .

JOYCE: Go to the toilet, Mother.

137. INT. CHILVERS' BATHROOM. NIGHT

*Pan down from bottles of shampoo, tins of talcum powder, in
clouds of steam, reclining in the bath, one leg delicately poised over*

the edge, is the dead PIG. MOTHER *looks at it from her seat on the toilet. Going to the door, she opens it to find the busy* NUTTALL *waiting, razor in hand.*

138. INT. CHILVERS' SITTING ROOM. NIGHT
LOCKWOOD *peeps through the curtains, watching the street. He nods.*
INSPECTOR NOBLE: Right. Off you go.
> (NUTTALL, *seen waiting for the word in the hall, leaves with* PRESTON.)

139. INT./EXT. WORMOLD'S CAR/CHILVERS' HOUSE. NIGHT
WORMOLD *becomes alert as he sees his quarry emerging. As* NUTTALL *drives off in his van,* WORMOLD *follows at a discreet distance.*

140. INT. CHILVERS' SITTING ROOM. NIGHT
LOCKWOOD *nods as he peeps through the curtains.*
DR SWABY: We'll wait five minutes. Get the pig ready. (*To* MOTHER) Do you have a hat and coat?
> (MOTHER *shrinks back in horror.*)
Think yourself very lucky, the pair of you. You've got off very lightly indeed.
ALLARDYCE: But he was fond of her. You were fond of her, I can tell. (*To* JOYCE) And don't be too upset. We're as much in the wrong as you are. If anybody found out about this we'd all be ruined.
> (*There is a silence, while the others turn to* ALLARDYCE.)
JOYCE: Oh really? I think you'd better sit down. I think we've got some talking to do.
GILBERT: Joyce.
JOYCE: Shut up. Sit down.
> (DR SWABY, LOCKWOOD, INSPECTOR NOBLE *and* ALLARDYCE *sit down.*)
DR SWABY: (*To* ALLARDYCE) Pillock.

JOYCE: Perhaps you'd like a little sherry now?
DR SWABY: Very well.
>   (JOYCE *smiles sweetly.*)

141. INT. CHILVERS' HALL. NIGHT
The front door is open. DR SWABY *and* ALLARDYCE *are on the point of leaving.*
JOYCE: Now you've found the way to our door, I hope you'll come again.
ALLARDYCE: (*Eagerly*) Yes, rather.
DR SWABY: I'm bound to say, Mrs Chilvers, you've gone up in my estimation. You've got more about you than your husband.
>   (*They step nimbly aside as* LOCKWOOD *and* INSPECTOR NOBLE *come smartly from the sitting room with the* PIG *in one of Mother's hats and a button overcoat. They go straight out the front door.* GILBERT *has followed them into the hall.*)
DR SWABY: And incidentally, if you ever want your mother put in a home I'm on the board of several.
JOYCE: Oh, how kind! *A bientôt.*
>   (*They go and she closes the door in triumph.*)
>   Well, Gilbert, I think sexual intercourse is in order.
>   (*She pushes him back into the sitting room and closes the door. At the top of the stairs,* MOTHER *looks out from her room. She comes down the stairs. She listens at the sitting-room door.*)
MOTHER: No pig. No pig.

142. EXT. HEWSON'S WIRELESS SHOP. DAY
A CROWD *watches the royal wedding on the tiny screen of the television in the shop window.* GILBERT, *passing on his bike, stops. He tries to peer over the crowd but those sitting on stepladders at the back defeat him.*

143. INT. ALLARDYCE'S SITTING ROOM. DAY
MRS ALLARDYCE *and* VERONICA *watch their television. They shush* ALLARDYCE *as he comes in.*

144. INT. MRS FORBES'S BEDROOM. EVENING
The radio is giving highlights of the wedding. MRS FORBES *is getting poshed up. She is staining her legs with gravy browning, to represent nylons.*

145. INT. WORMOLD'S ROOM. EVENING
WORMOLD *is sitting still. The room is quiet. A single light burning.*
MRS FORBES: *(Out of vision)* Are you busy?
WORMOLD: *(Warming)* No.
MRS FORBES: *(Out of vision)* Are you any good at painting?

146. INT. MRS FORBES'S BEDROOM. EVENING
MRS FORBES *stands on a table.* WORMOLD *has an eyebrow pencil in his hand.*
MRS FORBES: I wouldn't ask anybody to do this, only you're a professional man and we've been through a lot, one way and another.
WORMOLD: Shall I start at the bottom or the top?
MRS FORBES: Oh, it's perhaps better if you work your way up . . . Maurice.
(WORMOLD, *under some strain, begins to draw the seam up her leg. There is a knock at the door.*)
WORMOLD: *(Stopping)* There's somebody at the front door.
MRS FORBES: Take no notice. We're busy, aren't we?

147. EXT. MRS FORBES'S HOUSE. NIGHT
NUTTALL *waits at the front door in his finery. He is mystified. A call through the letterbox brings no joy. Giving the house a look, he walks away. Ahead of him, down the street, we see the hotel and the Town's Best arriving for the Dinner.*

148. INT. MRS FORBES'S BEDROOM. EVENING
WORMOLD'S *pencil passes over the back of her knee. He starts up the back of her thigh.*
WORMOLD: I love you, Mrs Forbes.

MRS FORBES: I wondered if you did.

WORMOLD: Will you marry me?

MRS FORBES: Possibly. Only I'm still waiting to hear from Kuala Lumpur. Anyway we can cross that t when we come to it. (*Pause.*) Mr Wormold.

WORMOLD: What?

MRS FORBES: You'll have to be less keen on your job.

WORMOLD: (*Lifting up her skirt slightly*) Shall I draw in the stocking tops?

149. INT. HOTEL FUNCTION ROOM. NIGHT
The Royal Wedding Dinner. Prominent on the top table is the PIG's *head, with an apple in its mouth.* DR *and* MRS SWABY, MR *and* MRS LOCKWOOD, MR *and* MRS ALLARDYCE *and* INSPECTOR NOBLE, *are also at the top table.* NUTTALL *has an*

empty place at his side. In a fairly lowly seating position we find GILBERT *and* JOYCE, *and even* MOTHER. *Sitting near them are the* SUTCLIFFS. *There is a good deal of coming and going behind them.*

JOYCE: They would put us right next door to the toilet. What are you doing?

GILBERT: Nothing, nothing.

(JOYCE *thinks she's seen him take something she'd left on the side of her plate.* MOTHER *is still eating, though most people have finished.*)

JOYCE: Still, toilet or no toilet, we're in now. In ten years time that'll be us.

(GILBERT *looks towards the fairly dispiriting collection of notables on the top table. He notices* ALLARDYCE *turn the* PIG's *head away.* ALLARDYCE *looks briefly at* GILBERT. DR SWABY *rises.*)

DR SWABY: My Lord Mayor, My Lady Mayoress, Ladies and Gentlemen, it is my great pleasure to propose to you now the toast of "The Happy Couple".

(*Everybody rises, except* MOTHER *who is still eating, and only a nudge from* JOYCE *fetches her to her feet. As they raise their glasses, a Brussels sprout rolls out unnoticed from* GILBERT's *serviette.*)

ALL: The Happy Couple.

150. INT. HOTEL FUNCTION ROOM. NIGHT
In the after-dinner dance, DR SWABY *and* JOYCE *make a handsome couple in the foxtrot. We notice that* DR SWABY's *hand wanders.*

151. INT./EXT. OLD RAILWAY WAGON. DAY
In another secret "sty", a chubby pink PIGLET *is being lovingly fed titbits by* GILBERT *and* ALLARDYCE. GILBERT *picks the* PIGLET *up, cradling it. End credits over this.*